THE **LIFE** AND **TIMES** OF **FRANK LIEBIG** AND **FRED HERRIG**

GLACIER COUNTRY 1902–1910

First Rangers

C. W. Guthrie

FARCOUNTRY PRESS

Dedicated to the memory of Frank Liebig,
Fred Herrig, and other first rangers.

ISBN: 978-1-56037-749-8

Cover image of Lake McDonald provided by pixabay.com.

Originally published as *The First Ranger: Adventures of a Pioneer Forest Ranger, Glacier Country, 1902-1910*, © 1995 by C. W. Guthrie, Redwing Publishing, Huson, Montana.

For more information about our books, write Farcountry Press, P.O. Box 5630, Helena, MT 59604; call (800) 821-3874; or visit www.farcountrypress.com.

Library of Congress Cataloging-in-Publication Data

Names: Guthrie, C. W., author.
Title: First rangers : adventures of a pioneer forest ranger, glacier country 1902-1910 / C.W. Guthrie.
Description: Helena, MT : Farcountry Press, [2019] | Includes bibliographical references.
Identifiers: LCCN 2019019849 | ISBN 9781560377498 (softcover)
Subjects: LCSH: Liebig, Frank, 1872-1950. | Herrig, Frederick, 1860-1939. | Forest rangers--Montana--Glacier National Park--Biography. | United States. Forest Service--Officials and employees--Biography.
Classification: LCC SD387.F6 G88 2019 | DDC 634.9092/2786 B--dc23 LC record available at https://lccn.loc.gov/2019019849

Produced and printed in the United States of America.

23 22 21 20 19 1 2 3 4 5

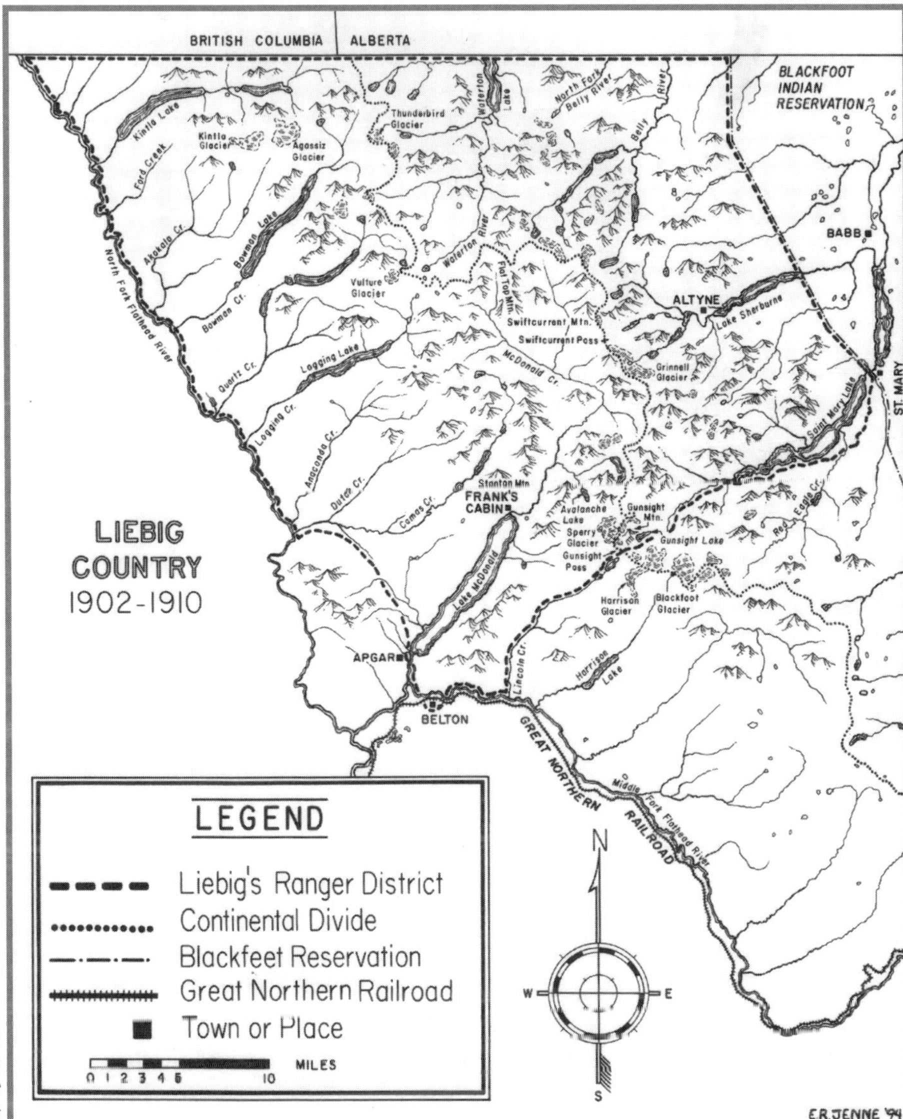

Map by E. R. Jenne

Now Glacier National Park, Montana

The whole country is yours, from Belton to Canada and across the Rockies to the prairie between Waterton Lake and the foot of Saint Mary Lake. You're to look for fires, timber thieves, squatters, and game violators. Go to it and Good Luck.

—Flathead Forest Reserve Supervisor
Fremont N. Haines

Frank Liebig crossing the South Fork of the Flathead River. LIEBIG COLLECTION.

ACKNOWLEDGMENTS

My thanks and appreciation to Jean Liebig Soldowski, Margaret Liebig, Frances Liebig, Carl Liebig, and Ted Soldowski for sharing their memories of their father and grandfather and for saving Frank's journals, stories, and photographs for the generations to come. Also, thanks to Don and Polly Bunger for recognizing Frank as an extraordinary man and taking notes along the trail back in the 1930s and for the hard work that went into Don's 1950 manuscript about those times. Heartfelt thanks are also due to Carl and Vi Wetterstrom for sharing their memories of Frank and Lulu and to Fred Herrig's daughter-in-law Inez Herrig and Fred's stepgrandchildren Herb Wilke and Frieda Wilke Miller for sharing their photographs and documents. Following the first printing of this book and in accordance with Inez Herrig's wishes, the original Roosevelt letters were donated to the Roosevelt Museum at the Sagamore Hill National Historic Site, New York. I greatly appreciated the advice of Jud Moore, E. G. Heilman, and Mark White of the U.S. Forest Service and the assistance of LeAnn Simpson and Wendy Hill of the Glacier Natural History Association. I'd like to thank E. R. Jenne for his illustrations and maps. Finally, special acknowledgment and appreciation goes to Linda Netschert, Kathy Springmeyer, Will Harmon, and the staff of Farcountry Press for publishing this new edition of *First Rangers*.

Sawing logs to build the ranger station, 1902. LIEBIG COLLECTION.

The above photograph is from the Liebig Collection, now housed in the Glacier National Park Archives. This ranger's version of an open-pit sawmill remained widely in use until the late 1800s. Note the handle on the bottom of the saw. That area was known as the *box;* the handle was used to pull the saw downward. The man leaning on the log on the left was probably the *box man* who always wore a big hat because of the shower of sawdust. The man at the top was known as the *tiller*. The other three men were helpers.

CONTENTS

Forest Ranger Frank Liebig at the Mount Stanton Ranger Station, 1907. LIEBIG COLLECTION.

INTRODUCTION

Over a hundred years ago, a young German came to the United States. He wanted no part of the cities, and acquiring wealth was never his goal. He came to live in the American wilderness. His journey, by necessity, was roundabout and it took longer than he had wished, but he steadily made his way to the Northwest, to the land of the glaciers. This was the land of legend to the people he left behind and it was the land of his youthful dreams. He climbed the mighty mountains, looked down upon the winding streams and shining lakes in the mountain-girded valleys below. He watched the eagles fly, idled in the sun, and occasionally had a short talk with his maker while he was in the neighborhood. He hunted the woods and fished the streams. At night he took pleasure in supper over an open campfire and in reading tales from a time-scarred book by the fire's glow. He felt at home in this glacial wilderness. It suited him, and by his reckoning he was welcome in it; he had not been swallowed by a silent waiting glacier, crushed by a falling tree, swatted senseless by a quick-tempered grizzly, or made a meal of by an outlaw lion. On occasion, the wind severely lashed him and the freezing cold hovered about making ominous threats, but this too he reckoned was a form of wilderness hospitality.

He followed the trails of elk and deer, and sheep and goats, and Cree and Blackfeet and Flathead Indians. He traveled over the paths of trappers and explorers and wandering prospectors. And he, as they had, made new trails through the thick forests and rugged mountains. His footprints are there in the hundreds of miles of trails he made from West Glacier to the Canadian border and across the Rockies to St. Mary's Lake. For a time, this man who loved and walked this wilderness was its guardian. Frank Liebig was the first forest ranger assigned to protect the wild and magnificent country of the glaciers *from fires, timber thieves, squatters, and game violators.*

Frank Liebig's comrade Fred Herrig was twelve years older than Frank and became a ranger two year earlier in the district west of Glacier country, and he kept a watchful eye on the area until Frank was assigned. Fred was as colorful a character as any in western lore, and he was a lifelong friend of Theodore Roosevelt. Frank Liebig and Fred Herrig are of that breed of men that Roosevelt described as "straight and square and game."

Forest rangers were required to keep a journal and make a report once a month. These journals are records of the ranger's daily activities and were sometimes jokingly referred to as "liar's diaries." A few early rangers told why—one time when they were either rained out or snowed in and unable to work, they sent in a report to that effect, then were promptly docked in pay for whatever time they were counted idle. So, they never sent in a report like that again. Hail, sleet, snow, or high water, the rangers' journals demonstrated that they worked every day.

Most of these journals are sparse in detail and Frank Liebig's is no exception. Written while in the saddle riding along the trail, leaning against a tree, or seated at a table in a dimly lit cabin, the journals record what he did but reveal little detail of the ceaseless labor, often against the raging wrath of nature, that he endured to do it. These daily hardships were matters of routine to these rangers and didn't require much mention. The stories that are passed on in this book in Frank's words, and the excerpts from his journals, are like him—stern, short on words, and humorously matter of fact.

Frank Liebig's first child, Jean, lived the first days of her life in the wilderness of the Flathead Forest Reserve. Her life as the child of this

Frank Liebig hiking into Swiftcurrent Pass, early 1900s. LIEBIG COLLECTION.

rugged ranger in the forests of the Rockies and later as a rural Montana schoolteacher is a fascinating piece of western history. Her story alone is worthy of telling, but she, as loving daughters will, wanted her father's story told, and she and her brother Carl and sisters Margaret and Frances have provided the documents, the pictures, and their own recollections of Frank for this work.

While reading through the numerous articles, journals, and letters they provided, I came across a draft of an unpublished biography by Don Bunger. Don met Frank in the summer of 1930 while working for the U.S. Forest Service and was "much impressed." He kept notes, and years later he wrote a biography but had never submitted it for publication. Don Bunger wrote about Frank Liebig with the respect one man has earned from another.

Fred Herrig's memorabilia was found stored in leather pouches in a shed by Fred's daughter-in-law, Inez Herrig, of Libby, Montana. Fred did not save much information about himself. Most of what was found was about Roosevelt and the Rough Riders.

This work is written from the letters and journals of Frank Liebig, memorabilia of Fred Herrig, excerpts from the works of Don Bunger, and the memories of Frank's children and Fred's daughter-in-law Inez Herrig and step-grandchildren Herb Wilke and Frieda Wilke Miller. Dialogue is derived from Frank and Fred's written accounts or from their stories as passed on to their children.

Don Bunger gave his reasons for writing his 1950 manuscript about Frank. This work is written for the same reason.

> *These stories are rare bits of history, which need to be gathered into one place and preserved for the nature lover, the hunter, the outdoorsman, and the whole population of this great nation. They will never happen again to anyone, for the conditions are not here anymore to produce them.*

ONE

CALL OF THE WILDERNESS

Frank was destined to rove, to leave the love of kin, the comfort of the familiar, and the velvet caress of a known fate. And he was not a man to do things by half. He would shed one life and begin an unknown other. He had read of places and mountains and trees that staggered the mind to see. They beckoned from across the seas.

Young Frank

Frank's father, Karl Liebig, and his uncles, Wilhelm and Albert, and cousin Louis were among the young Prussian men who made up Chancellor Bismarck's efficient military machine of the 1860s that defeated Austria and Denmark and finally France in 1870. These victories gave birth to the powerful German Empire in 1871. By then, Chancellor Bismarck had united Prussia with the South German States of Bavaria, Wurttemberg, Thuringia, and Saxony. Bismarck annexed the French provinces of Alsace and Lorraine and made them a part of the German Empire as well. Bismarck also forged alliances with Russia, Austria, and Italy for resources. This access to new resources, combined with the German natural ability to turn science into productive uses, catapulted Germany into becoming the industrial giant of Europe.

When the wars were over, the weary Liebig men came home. They took up their professions, married, and began their families.

McDonald Creek above Avalanche Creek, Continental Divide in distance. LIEBIG COLLECTION.

On August 2, 1872, the first son of Karl and Louise Liebig was born. He arrived, wailing with good health, at their home in Eberswalde, Germany. They named this first son Franz Friedreich Liebig to honor Karl's father and a fallen comrade of the wars.

Franz, nicknamed Frank, lived his first eighteen years in Bismarck's prospering German Empire. His father had returned to his trade of millwright and built sawmills in the forests throughout Germany, Poland, and Switzerland. His uncles and cousins were millwrights, carpenters, and woodsmen and always lived nearby. The family moved several times, but Frank's childhood was spent mostly around Freiburg near the Black Forest in the south and in northeastern Germany at his birthplace in Eberswalde, south of the Baltic Sea near Berlin. They lived in the countryside, in quaint, neighborly hamlets with narrow cobble streets and gray stone houses brightened in the spring by well-tended window boxes of brilliant red and yellow and white flowers. His mother, Louise, kept their modest homes spick and span, smelling of fresh hot breads, sweet pastries, and simmering soups.

When Frank was two, Louise gave birth to a girl and shortly created a Liebig family mystery that remains unsolved to this day. The infant daughter, whom they had named Heldvig, was adopted out to the Shroeder family of which little is known. Only Karl and Louise knew the reason they turned their first daughter over to the Shroeders to raise as their own, and they kept their secret through the years amidst probing family speculation and village gossip. Frank was four when his brother Max was born, ten when young Karl was born, and seventeen when his sister Frieda came along.

During the time of Germany's prospering years and until about 1890, daily life had become decidedly better for many Germans. Royalty and the landed gentry benefitted most by the nation's prosperity, and the factory workers and shop keepers in the cities also fared very well, but the Liebig's were among the German peasantry and the oppressed of the Empire. Although they lived a short distance north of the center of the great power struggles and political intrigue and in the shadow of the sprawling growth of German industries, their lives were little changed by Germany's prospering years, except that the government was not as aggressive in calling up the young working men to serve in the military during this time of peace and progress.

The Liebigs represented a long line of outdoorsmen and they pursued the professions that kept them in the hills and the cool green forests. They choked on the notion of going into the cities and working in the confinement of the factories or a science laboratory. One notable exception was their distant cousin Baron von Justus Liebig, a chemist who discovered chloral and revealed the importance of nitrogen and carbon dioxide in plant growth and for whom the Liebig laboratory condenser is named.

The Liebigs were steady, quiet, men and well-known experts in their crafts. They toiled proudly, feeling the good sweat of hard labor and the exhilaration and satisfaction of work well done. But simmering deep within was a longing for the freedoms, adventures, and opportunities they heard existed elsewhere in the world for men of their status. At night, when their hard day's labor was finished, Karl, Wilhelm, Albert, and Louis sat around the warmth of the fire talking about America. Young Frank sat among them as they read letters from the families of distant cousins who had immigrated to Pennsylvania in 1817 and from old family friends who had journeyed even farther west. He listened intently, intrigued by the stories they spun about the wonderful lives they would lead in such a country of freedoms. They boasted, with hearty laughter, about what grand marks they would make on civilization and what wonderful adventures they would have in the giant untouched forests. Although the desire for the American adventure ran deep in all the Liebigs, Frank would be the only one of his family to leave Germany and take his chances in the new country.

In the Liebig family, as with most German families, work came before play. Even the very young had duties, partly to share the daily family chores and partly to mold the German character of obedience and diligence at work, which was the measure of their worth and the justification of their existence. As a very small boy, Frank was responsible for tending the family geese. Each morning, he drove the flock to the pastures outside of the village and stood guard while they pecked at the bugs and grains and grasses in the ground, making a great show of swallowing their food. He idled away the time watching as they dashed here and there, flapping their wings and hissing threats at each other in some social order he did not understand. In the afternoon, he herded the flock of geese back to town where they drank and splashed in the water that ran fresh from the hills through the streets. When the geese had satisfied themselves and began to preen their feathers, he put them safely away in a pen in the tiny yard at the back of their house. Only then was he allowed to play with the other children of the village.

In the summer, the children waded barefoot in the cool, running waters. They sailed their homemade boats of wood and paper along the streets. Whenever there was more than one boy and one boat, a race was on. The race was immediately followed by pushing and shoving and a noisy, name-calling fracas over which boat really came in first and was the true champion of the day. In winter, when the water in the

Frank Liebig viewing the Garden Wall from Granite Park. LIEBIG COLLECTION.

streets had turned to ice, the children skated through the narrow streets of the village and on the ponds nearby, mastering a necessary skill for living in the German countryside. When Frank's father was home from building sawmills in the forests, the two of them went into the hills where he learned to ski. Skiing, like ice skating, was often the only way to travel from village to village in the winter.

The national pastime for boys in Germany was bouncing buttons, just as playing marbles was in America. The walls of the houses were built straight up from the sidewalks. Every boy carried his pockets full of buttons, and wherever there was a smooth wall and a sidewalk, generally there was a game in progress. They threw the buttons against the wall. Whoever's buttons bounced back nearest to the line won all the other buttons. Frank was a skilled player with a fat cache of buttons and a worthy reputation among his playmates.

At six, Frank went to a public school in Eberswalde and graduated at fourteen. He was expected to follow in his father's footsteps and become a millwright so was sent to the School of Mechanics in Landsberg am Lech for six months. He returned home to learn the millwright trade and the operation of sawmills from his father.

He went with his father on long trips across Germany, Poland, and Switzerland. At fifteen, he was a strong, wiry youth and a skilled hand at helping his father set up a sawmill. He had inherited good mechanical sense, and his father taught him about leverage and fulcrums as he became skilled in lifting and setting the big saws in place. The functions of wheels, cogs, and cables came easy to him, and he enjoyed fitting them together into a smoothly rotating force that moved the heavy logs onto chutes and into the teeth of the giant saws. When his first mill was up and running, he stood by, smiling through a rainfall of sawdust, as the screeching grinding saw cut logs into boards for houses and furniture. It was a satisfying profession, and he was becoming a fine craftsman. His father was justly proud. Karl Liebig and son would make a great team of millwrights, and Karl made plans for the two of them that stretched far into the future.

As Frank and his father traveled from forest to forest setting up sawmills, Frank began to realize that no matter how well he performed the craft of constructing with woods and metals, he was much more interested in the living trees and in the forest life that surrounded them. He made an effort to get acquainted with the forest officials who were assigned to care and manage the forests and monitor the progress of the sawmills. He asked a million questions and would not let up until he had answers. They took a liking to him and began teaching him about the different species of trees, which trees grew the fastest, and which produced the best lumber. He became fascinated with learning what elements of the forest lands caused some trees of the same species to grow oddly large and dominate the others, like Kaisers of the forest, and some to remain hearty but slow-growing replicas of their bigger neighbors. He began to learn about the wildlife—the fox, deer, bear, birds, fish, insects, plants, and the soil and how each part of the living forest was medicine for the other parts. His father and uncles had taught him the knack of creating sheltered comfort in pouring rains, deep snows, and the dark isolation of shadowy forests. The forest officials added some tricks of their own to his knowledge about how to survive in the woods. He was fast becoming a skilled woodsman.

> *My father was a millwright, more or less by trade, and established sawmills all over the worked areas in Eastern Prussia and Poland, he wanted me to learn the trade. But the more I came in contact with Forest Officers, the more I became convinced that the sawmill trade was not to my liking. So, I went as an apprentice under an old hand, on a big estate that carried a good many thousand acres of mixed stand of hardwood and some pine. My duties were to help in the planting crews and collect beetles in ditches that were constructed around newly planted areas—also to put a number on all cord wood that was worked up every summer from windfall and look after grazing stock and game.*

Through the centuries, the German royalty regarded the wooded lands, fowl, and game as exceedingly precious, rivaling the American notions about gold and oil. Most of the forested lands were either under the control of royal descendants or the wealthy landed gentry.

Montana's first oil rig, Kintla Lake region. GLACIER NATIONAL PARK ARCHIVES.

Lands that would have been considered public lands in America were the Kaiser's lands in Germany. Although great portions of the land of the German Empire were heavily wooded, they were mere remnants of the forests of centuries past. The thick stands of trees were slim poles and game scarce. The landowners and the Kaiser were strict and stingy about their woodlands, lest the growing populations think they were entitled to freely use and eventually deplete the riches of these fragile lands. The resourceful German landowners also took measures to conserve and restore the forests for their continued wood products and their own prosperity. Stumps were cut low and a new tree was planted whenever an older tree was cut. All waste wood was cut into firewood and sold to the highest bidder. The money received for the wood helped to pay the salaries of the foresters, and the costs of protecting the forest from game and fish poachers. Game hunting was contracted to one man and only he was allowed to hunt in that area and only for the game that was specified in his contract. The money from these contracts also helped pay the salaries of the forester, fishing was contracted the same way. Each stream was seined with nets of a specified size to allow the smaller fish to escape. Only the man with the contract could fish the area. Under these strict rules, only the man with a contract could hunt or fish.

Frank was an ordinary man and someday would be a forester, but he was not so well-stationed as to hope that he would someday get a contract that would permit him to hunt or fish at his will. It was unlikely that he would ever be privileged to freely feed himself with the fish and game of his country or to test his skills in the wild. The restrictions imposed on him by his country did not sit well. Frank had grown up listening to the fireside talk about America. He had read the eloquent descriptions of the wondrous new country and savored the tales of tribulations and successes. He knew that beyond Germany, beyond Europe, beyond the Atlantic, there were giant trees, great mountains, lands that were free, and wild game of all kinds, and even the ordinary man could hunt and fish. He would not just dream about going to America as the others dreamed. *He would go.*

When Frank was sixteen, Emperor-Kaiser Wilhelm II acceeded to the throne of Germany. Wilhelm resented Chancellor Bismarck's power and popularity so he instituted flamboyant and oppressive policies to disrupt Bismarck's hold on the German people and establish his own authority in Europe. But Wilhelm could not outdo the shrewd Bismarck, and in 1890 he dismissed him and put the chancellery into pliable but less able hands. This act would change Germany and eventually upend the world. The great German Empire began its decline.

Frank's resolve to go to America had never wavered, but when the prosperous Germany began to decline he worried that he would be put out of work or called into military service before he had earned enough money to make the trip. But luck was with him, and by 1895, when he was twenty-three, he had saved enough to make the journey.

On a cool, cloudy September day, he stuffed his clothes into a duffel, pulled on new boots, a wool coat, and his tired old hat. His weeping mother busied herself in the kitchen packing food for his journey to the ship that would take him away. His proud father paced the floor in another room. Karl had set aside his hopes that his eldest son would join him in the millwright trade when Frank turned to forestry. Now he was forced to let go of his naturally held expectation that his eldest son would be near to succeed him and head the Liebig family when the time came, just as he had done for his father and all the first sons had done before him. Karl was grievously disappointed, but he stiffened himself and joined Wilhelm and Albert and Louis and the heavyhearted Max and young Karl and the tearful Louise and Frieda, who had gathered around Frank near the doorway for a last farewell. There was no holding Frank. It was useless to try. Karl took Frank's hand in a firm, lingering handshake that they both would always remember. It was their final goodbye. Frank would never look back as he walked the 250 kilometers to the port at Hamburg to get passage on the SS *Prussia* to New York. As he later recalled:

> *I never finished my forestry course, as I received some glowing reports in letters from some friends in the good old U.S.A. I got the wanderlust and by a miracle I escaped the German Military Service and came across the pond, to Grand Island, Nebraska.*

The Liebig family had an old friend who had immigrated to America some years before and settled in Nebraska. They wrote often and, hearing of young Frank's unyielding desire to come to the USA, invited him to come to their farm and served as his sponsor, giving him tips about getting through the wearisome immigration process. He got off the crowded ship at Ellis Island, and after a tense, tiring wait, he cleared customs and officially entered the United States. He broke away from the dazed, wandering immigrants who had journeyed with him and headed straight for the New York train station. He motioned to the busy passing people for help in reading the schedule boards and found a gentleman to translate his German into English and assist while he purchased tickets for the westbound trains.

Frank found a job in Grand Island, Nebraska, working on a ranch feeding cattle for fifteen dollars a month and board. He went to school at night to learn the English language and get some American education.

Soon after he finished his schooling, he made friends with a man going to the west coast and decided to go with him. It was there, along the Washington and Oregon coast, that he saw the trees of his youthful visions. *The size of which made the trees of Germany look like fishing poles.* He worked about a year on the coast for the Washougal Logging Company, surveying logging roads, constructing chutes, and building a dam. He liked being in the trees, but he didn't like the rainy, foggy weather and wandered back into the interior of the States.

By good fortune, he got a job with the McNamara and Marlow Ranch near Big Sandy along the Missouri River and close to the badlands. Frank took naturally to the harsh life of a cowboy. He bucked the fierce prairie winds without complaint, rode herd for hours, and worked as many hours as it took to irrigate alfalfa and timothy; gather the hay for winter feed; mend fences; rope, brand, dehorn, and castrate young bulls; and drive the range-fattened steers to the trains that would take them to the markets in the East. In winter, he patched up barns and sheds and fixed ranch equipment. In a short time, he had become a good horseman and a skilled, reliable ranch hand. His hard work won him favor, and McNamara and Marlow made him the foreman of the ranch.

Frank was doing well. He liked being an American cowboy. He enjoyed the work and the camaraderie of nights around a campfire or in a bunkhouse swapping stories with the other cowhands. He had settled into what he thought was a good job, on a good spread, for some *darn nice people.* But his desire to live in the forested wilderness was like a tight cinch around his soul. After three years, he quit his job as ranch foreman and drifted on.

> *I didn't like this country as there was not enough timber to suit me, so I went back to the west side of the Rockies and stopped at Belton, Montana, to look around. This was in August 1900. Incidentally, the Great Northern Depot at that time was a derailed boxcar. Here in Belton a small oil boom was in progress. Some parties had found oil seepage around the Kintla Lakes on the North Fork of the Flathead River not far from the Canadian boundary line. Some men from Butte were in Belton, going up to the Kintla Lakes to take up oil claims. The people hired me to survey out their claims, which I did for four months.*

Lake McDonald in 1900. PHOTOGRAPHS BY FRANK LIEBIG. LIEBIG COLLECTION.

Glacier Country

When Frank arrived in Glacier country in 1900, the copper, silver, and gold mining booms of 1898 east of the Continental Divide in Swiftcurrent, Java, and Divide Creeks were at their pitiful peaks. The boomtown of Altyn had mushroomed into existence near the head of Sherburne Lake. It was a rough, rip-roaring town of western legend, with stores, saloons, cabins and tents, miners, gamblers, and whores. It was a town of consequence, boasting at least one issue of a town newspaper. By 1902, the toiling miners would grow fed up with the meager treasures the spectacular country would offer up for their hell-hard labor. They would pack their shovels and picks and head for the Klondike, and Altyn would dwindle to a near ghost town.

Meanwhile, west of the divide, a roaming miner found oil seepage in the Kintla Lake region, spurring the interest of some Butte businessmen and setting off a small oil boom. Frank surveyed and staked out the claims up and down the valley and wrote up the required paperwork for fifty dollars a month and board. When he finished marking claims for the day and was back in the bustling Kintla camp, he watched with idle interest as crude shacks and Montana's first oil rig went up.

> *After that period, I quit the company and went on my own hook, even took up oil claims in the Belly River on the east side of the Rocky Mountains. I made this trip to the head of Lake McDonald*

by canoe, thence walked up McDonald Creek for ten miles, thence Mineral Creek to the head, and, crossing the Chaney Glacier, hit the head of the Middle Fork of the Belly River, as far as Glens Lake and the Canadian boundary. I made the foot of Lake McDonald my headquarters.

Frank built a cabin near the west shore at the foot of the lake. Then he roamed the country as he had always wanted to do. He invested in a camera and took pictures along the way. He forded the cold, fast-running streams and paddled his canoe across the vast, shimmering lakes. He spent long, fascinating days exploring the majestic peaks and deep valleys and making his way across the ice-age glaciers and through the thick, forbidding forests. He hunted and fished for his food and made enough off of his Belly River claims to provide himself with clothes and staples. Frank was content with his life as a mountain man. This is what he came to America to do, and he thought he would do it forever, but it was not to be.

Far right is Frank Liebig. Standing next to him is Albert "Death on the Trail" Reynolds, who later became a park ranger, and two assistants, 1905. GLACIER NATIONAL PARK ARCHIVES.

TWO

FOREST RANGERS AND RANGE RIDERS

The first of them, the ones that made good, were rugged and honorable men, and they had the best of life's game. They had some power, some pay, and some glory. There were no volumes of written rules on how to do the job that choked out their own worthy thoughts or muddled their judgment. They were good men, deciding how a good job should be done as they went about it. They were the law, the trailblazer, the fireman. Their tasks often called for backbreaking labor in dangerous situations, and they never had a dull day. They lived and labored in an Eden, and always another spirit-stirring challenge lay just ahead. How grand it must have been!

In 1891, Congress approved an "Act to repeal timber-culture laws, and for other purposes," which authorized the president of the United States to set apart public lands bearing forests, whether of commercial value or not, as public reservations. Six years later, in 1897, President Grover Cleveland issued proclamations establishing the Flathead and Lewis and Clark Forest Reserves in northern Montana. But it was not until 1901, when Theodore Roosevelt became president, ten years after the timber-culture repeal act and four years after the Flathead and Lewis and Clark Reserves were established, that there were any serious attempts to preserve the resources and natural beauty of these lands from the juggernaut of ambitious investors, invading land developers, and impulsive settlers.

Early Lake McDonald settler, John D. (Jack) Reuter, who briefly moonlighted as a forest range rider. GLACIER NATIONAL PARK ARCHIVES.

Gifford Pinchot was appointed chief of the Division of Forestry in 1898. He had studied the problems in the forests of Europe and had seen the consequences to the European people of the declining forest resources. He was also a friend of Theodore Roosevelt and had a strong ally when the "*conservation president*" succeeded to office following the assassination of William McKinley in September 1901. Teddy would squeeze some legislation and money out of the nearsighted Congress to free the renamed Bureau of Forestry to act and to put men on the job.

The first supervisor in the Flathead Forest Reserve of 1897 was William J. "Tin Plate Bill" Brennan. He earned his name making speeches advocating tariffs on tin. Brennan took a sporting approach to protecting the forests. He was congenial, had a multitude of interests, and trumpeted many a public issue, but he did little to enforce the policies of the Forest Reserves. When the administration changed,

Brennan was replaced with the more serious-minded Fremont N. Haines. Haines was described as an Easterner who couldn't find his way around an orchard, which was true of many of the politically appointed forest supervisors. But Haines was willing to learn and was well liked. He had been handed a tough job by a determined chief of forestry, and he needed good men in the field.

In the first days of the reserve, the rangers were known as forest range riders and consisted of men who moonlighted at the job. They were saloonkeepers, ranchers, waiters, and blacksmiths, and men who loved grand adventures such as Indian scouts and rodeo cowboys. Jack Reuter, a settler at Belton, and C. F. Van Allen at Essex both moonlighted as forest range riders in 1901. The following year, Frank Liebig would be designated the first forest ranger in the Glacier District east of the North Fork of the Flathead River.

Fred Herrig, Range Rider and Forest Ranger

Before Jack Reuter, C. F. Van Allen, and Frank Liebig, there was Fred Herrig, a Spanish-American War veteran who had been assigned in 1900 as the range rider for the Upper North Fork of the Flathead Forest

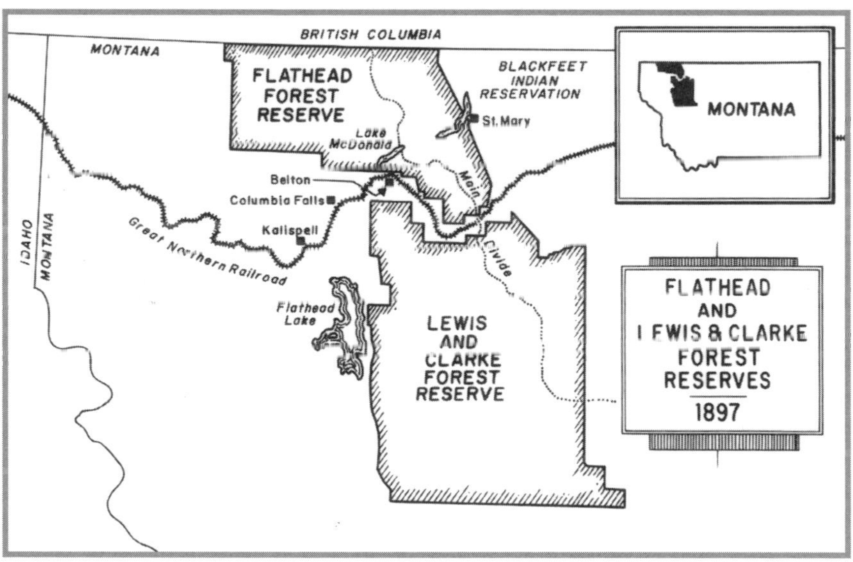

Map by E. R. Jenne

Map of the Flathead and Lewis & Clark Forest Reserves.

Reserve and whose patrols often spilled over into the country that would later become Glacier National Park.

Fred Herrig was born in Alsace-Lorraine in 1860 and came to America in 1875 when he was fifteen years old. Alsace was a mixture of German and French peoples. Chancellor Bismarck had made Alsace and part of Lorraine a part of the German Empire when Fred was eleven years old, but Fred always referred to himself as Alsatian and as French.

During his early years in the West, Fred hunted and trapped in British Columbia to make a living then turned to the life of a cowboy. In 1883, he hired on as a wrangler for the Marquis de Mores of France on the Marquis's cattle ranch on the Little Missouri River in the badlands of North Dakota.

The Marquis was the scion of a noble French family and a soldier of fortune. He had heard of the profits in the packing industry, and when he saw the huge herds of cattle in Montana and the Dakotas he devised a plan to build a packing and refrigerating plant in the midst of the cattle range and ship the products East.

The Marquis pitched a tent near the banks of the Little Missouri River, broke a bottle of champagne over the tent pole, and said that this was to be the town of Medora, named for his wife, and the site of a meat-packing venture that would give Armour and Swift a run for their money in the beef business. He built a slaughterhouse and homes and a store for the workmen, and the town of Medora began to emerge. Nearby he built up a vast ranch, bought up herds of cattle, and hired a foreman and several ranch hands. Fred was in charge of the horses and worked for the Marquis for about three years.

One day, Fred and a few of the other de Mores cowhands were hanging around town idling away the afternoon when the new owner of the Elkhorn and Chimney Butte Ranches south of Medora came riding in. He was from New York and everybody in town sized him up as a grassy tenderfoot. He went by the name of Theodore Roosevelt.

> *'Twas in Medora, in front of Joe Ferris's store, that a lot of us planned a little surprise for Mr. Roosevelt. He looked like a kid. I believe he was only a little past twenty, and what with his eye-glasses and his*

A young Fred Herrig. GLACIER NATIONAL PARK ARCHIVES.

knee-breeches and his little brown mustache, he did look too nice for anything. While he was in Joe Ferris' buying postage stamps, Will Dow, who afterwards worked along with me on the ranch, and a cowboy named Merrifield, and myself, unsaddled Roosevelt's pony, led him off and put the saddle and bridle on a bronco that was a dead ringer for his mount. We knew all about that bronco, for he'd already thrown Hell-roaring Bill Jones once that morning. So, we kinder sidled off to see the fun. By and by Roosevelt came out of the shop and started to mount. He was nearsighted, but he couldn't have told those cayuses apart anyway.

The bronco let him get into the saddle and then the beast bunched his feet and humped his back and Roosevelt went off, as easy as you please. Nobody said anything except Joe Ferris, who came out of the door and asked if he was hurt.

"Not a bit of it" said Roosevelt and up he went again. But the White-faced Kid, that's what we called the bronco, didn't wait for him to get his right foot in the leathers this time before he pitched the young fellow right over his head. It was the all-firedest jolt I ever saw. Roosevelt turned a somersault and then sat down so hard his glasses broke. Will Dow and I went to help him up. Merrifield was laughing so he couldn't move. Roosevelt didn't notice any of us. He just looked kinder surprised as he scrambled up—the dust was four inches thick in the road. "It's too bad I broke my glasses," said he and he limped into the store. We thought he had enough of it and were wondering how we could change nags again, when the tenderfoot came out with a new pair of glasses he'd fished out of his hand-bag and blast my eyes if he didn't jump up on the Kid's back again, and so quick this time the bronco didn't feel him till he'd got both feet in the stirrups and a good grip with his knees. It was the White-faced Kid that was surprised this time and they went off lickety-split in a cloud of dust.

There were only about eleven inhabitants in the town then, and it wasn't long until the news got out that the White-faced Kid was murdering a tenderfoot. We held a mass meeting in front of Ferris's store and when the overland train from the East pulled in and another tenderfoot got off and asked for his friend, Mr. Roosevelt, and said his name was Dr. Lambert and he came from New York. We said his friend Mr. Roosevelt was just about needing a doctor, and bad, too. But before we could explain, lickety-split through the dust came the White-faced Kid and there on his back, with all his teeth showing, was the doctor's friend, Roosevelt.

When Roosevelt clapped his peepers on Dr. Lambert, he let out a whoop that couldn't have been beat by any cowboy on the Little Missouri. We took a shine to him from that very day. Any fellow who could ride White-faced Kid at one trial and holler like that was the man for our money; except that we didn't have any money—until we'd hired out to Roosevelt.

One of Fred's duties on the Marquis de Mores's ranch was to accompany and protect the Marquis's wife, Medora de Mores, when she went horseback riding in the rugged country of the Badlands. One day when they were out riding, Medora's horse spooked, flinging her into the air and onto a cactus. Fred roared with laughter. He laughed until his belly hurt and he almost fell out of the saddle. He couldn't stop himself, although he wasn't much trying. The angrier the Marquise Medora de Mores became, the more helpless he was with laughter. When Fred and Medora returned to the ranch, the still furious Medora gave her enraged report to her husband. The Marquis's reaction to Medora's tale of picking herself up, pulling thorns from her fanny and climbing aboard her horse, while his paid wrangler sat on his horse doubled over with laughter was to fire Fred on the spot.

Still chuckling, Fred mounted up and went looking for another job. He found work on Teddy Roosevelt's Chimney Butte Ranch. This ranch was known by the locals as the Maltese Cross Ranch because of the eight-pointed Maltese Cross brand used on the stock. It was one of two ranches Roosevelt purchased in the Dakotas. The other ranch was the Elkhorn Ranch.

It turned out later that the Marquis, who was impulsive and known as a man of action, was also a man of very poor judgment. Through a series of bad deals with the railroad, the local cattlemen, and the butchers in the East, the packing plant went out of business. For a while he devoted himself to just raising cattle and then returned to France and was on to other adventures.

In September 1893, Roosevelt's New York friend, Dr. Lambert, was coming out for a big hunt, and Roosevelt sent word to Fred Herrig to come to work on the Elkhorn Ranch as a hunting guide.

That was as pretty a place as you ever saw, right on the bank of the Little Missouri, with a wide valley on the other side and then a range of sharp cliffs that cut off the view. The house was one story high, of squared logs, but there were plenty of rooms in it, big easy chairs on the porch and buffalo and bear skins all over the floors. As for wild game—well, you can get lost for three days even now in the triangle cut off by the Little Missouri, and the Big Missouri and the Northern Pacific Railroad.

Hell-roaring Bill Jones had went to work for Roosevelt. You see, Bill had been chief of police in Bismarck, North Dakota, and he and the mayor had words one day. Bill pulled his gun, he was too much of a gentleman to shoot the mayor, so he batted him over the head with the butt end of the pistol. That ended the argument. But after that the mayor said he thought Bill had better resign, so he passed in his badge and came to Medora. And when he heard of the tenderfoot who had tamed White-faced Kid, Bill said he guessed he was the kind of man he'd like to work for. By the time I went to work there, Bill was foreman of the Elkhorn Ranch, and Sylvane Ferris, Joe Ferris' brother, was head cowboy.

Bill and Sylvane had stayed sober all summer so's to be O.K. for the big hunt.

Doc Lambert mounted Sorrel Joe. Roosevelt straddled Muley. Bill rode Tom, and I drove the White-faced Kid and Jim in the wagon. Roosevelt said it wasn't any fun to ride the Kid any more, since he'd pull to harness. Our third day out we saw antelope. "There's a big bull, but he's six hundred yards off," said Bill Jones when we first caught sight of the game. But the doctor hadn't got used to a country where distances are so deceiving. In that high dry air, the pronghorn didn't look, to a New York man, farther off than across Madison Square. As I was saying, the doctor paid no attention when Bill said the bull was six hundred yards off, but just blazed away with his 45-90. He missed the antelope by a hundred and fifty yards, shot that far short of him. Then the doctor played Fourth of July with the critter, shooting half dozen shells at him. He didn't hit the beast, either, which was not strange at the distance, but his fusillade turned the game off towards Roosevelt. And I never saw a prettier piece of work in my life than he did then with his rifle. It was just the same caliber as the doctor's. When Roosevelt pulled the trigger twice, at three hundred and twenty-five yards, the bull keeled over with one ball through his side and the other through his chest.

I saw Roosevelt get a fine sheep one day. He and Bill and I were sitting on the porch, taking it easy, when Bill says "I saw a sheep's track up on that butte yesterday." Pointing to the range right in front of us, across the valley. A Rocky Mountain sheep is about the rarest game we get there. Bill had no more than got the words out of his mouth when something poked its head up over the edge of the cliff. "There's the sheep now," says Roosevelt. "No, I believe it's a black-tailed antelope and I've a mind to go after him."

"Black-tailed nothing," said Bill. "That's the whitest tailed antelope you ever saw."

By this time, Roosevelt was creeping up the river with his rifle. We sat still and watched him. The air was calm and clear as a bell, and when he was a half mile off he could hear every word we said. "He ought to keep to the left and climb that coulee," said Bill, never thinking Roosevelt would hear him. But he did keep to the left and began crawling up the butte, which was all fluted with gullies. "Gimme them opery glasses," said Bill. He always called Roosevelt's field-glasses opery glasses—and just then Roosevelt fired. That was enough for us, and Bill and I went after him as hard as we could.

"Did you get your antelope?" called Bill, as Roosevelt stuck his head up from behind a boulder.

"It's a sheep!" yelled Roosevelt, pushing the critter up over the rock in front of him. "It's a sheep, by George, and I shot him through the heart."

My last hunt with Roosevelt was late in November. I guess he and I remember it mainly because we both froze our ears getting home to the ranch. He was anxious to kill a mountain ram before he went back East. It's all right to shoot Rocky Mountain sheep, but a whacking big ram, with horns spread like all out doors is different. So, we both made up our minds, he must have a ram, and started early in the morning over the divide between the Yellowstone and the Little Missouri rivers. By that time of year, the bunch grass was so brown you couldn't tell it from the rocks. The country looked about as desolate as you can imagine. The buttes raised their jagged edges against a cold gray sky and the only color in the landscape was in the sandstone and porphyry strata of the cliffs. We had a hard time of it making our way up to the crest of the divide, and just as we got there, along toward evening, I saw something moving ahead of us. "Easy now," says I, "and you'll get your ram."

"Where?" says he, and I could see by his voice he was all on thorns. We had worked hard for this very chance. He had his 45-90 rifle swinging easy over his left arm. I pointed about four hundred yards in front of us a little down ridge. It was one of the finest rams I ever saw, his long brown hair so much lighter in color than a ewe's, that he stood out tolerably plain even among the boulders at that distance.

I was just pointing the critter out when he faced about, lifted his big horns over a rock he'd been grazing behind, and caught sight of us against the skyline. "There he goes," I yelled, for 'twas no use keeping quiet any longer. Maybe that ram didn't run. But Roosevelt had seen him from the first jump and had his gun going. Spat, went a bullet against the sandstone. "Too far to the left," I yelled. Biff, the next one, quicker than I can tell it, knocked up the dust almost under the ram's feet. "Now's your chance," said I, for the beast had been running almost parallel with the crest of the range, and I was afraid every second he'd plunge down the bluff and we'd lose him. With that the rifle cracked once more, and that time I didn't see where the ball struck. But I did see the ram jump into the air, headed straight down the bluff and disappear. When we got to where we lost him, fearing to find he'd made one of those gigantic leaps down a precipice that the big horns are fond of in an emergency, Roosevelt gave a yell you could have heard two miles. The ram lay ten feet down the cliff, on a little shelf of rock, half over the edge and half propped against a dwarf pine. He was stone dead and we got the finest pair of horns I ever saw off him.

It was after midnight when we got home that night and we were happy even if our ears were frozen. "We can get new skin on our ears," said Roosevelt "but we'll never get another ram like that one."

Fred worked at the Elkhorn Ranch about five years. During one of Roosevelt's long absences from the ranch, Fred decided to mosey on. He was working as a packer, leading out strings of mules loaded with ore, and picking up his mail in Pleasant Valley, Montana, when Roosevelt telegraphed him from Washington, D.C. in 1898.

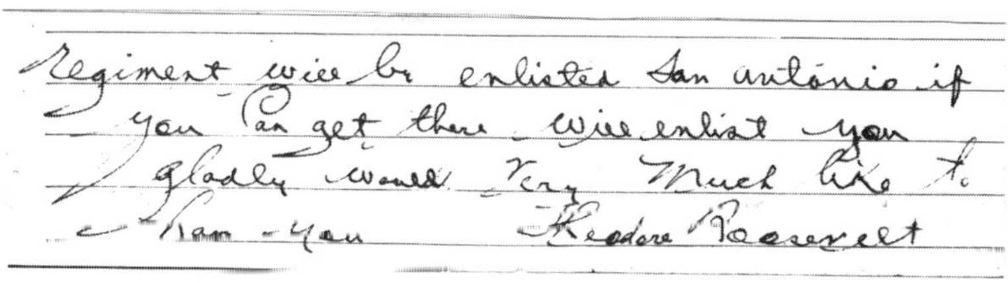
Regiment will be enlisted San Antonio if you can get there will enlist you gladly would very much like to have you Theodore Roosevelt

HERRIG FAMILY COLLECTION.

Roosevelt invited Herrig to enlist in the Rough Riders. (In 1996, the Herrig family donated the original Theodore Roosevelt letters printed in this book to the Roosevelt Museum at Sagamore Hill National Historic Site. The letters were also used in the 1999 television program, *The American Presidents,* which aired on the Public Broadcasting System.)

Fred was off to Cuba, war, and glory with Roosevelt's Rough Riders.

Fred was assigned to Troop K in the First Cavalry and fought at Las Guasimas, San Juan, and the siege of Santiago. He was breveted as a

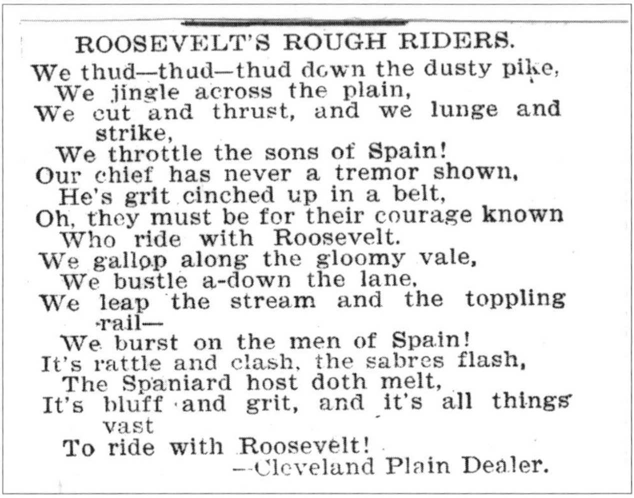

ROOSEVELT'S ROUGH RIDERS.

We thud—thud—thud down the dusty pike,
We jingle across the plain,
We cut and thrust, and we lunge and strike,
We throttle the sons of Spain!
Our chief has never a tremor shown,
He's grit cinched up in a belt,
Oh, they must be for their courage known
Who ride with Roosevelt.
We gallop along the gloomy vale,
We bustle a-down the lane,
We leap the stream and the toppling rail—
We burst on the men of Spain!
It's rattle and clash, the sabres flash,
The Spaniard host doth melt,
It's bluff and grit, and it's all things vast
To ride with Roosevelt!
—Cleveland Plain Dealer.

HERRIG FAMILY COLLECTION.

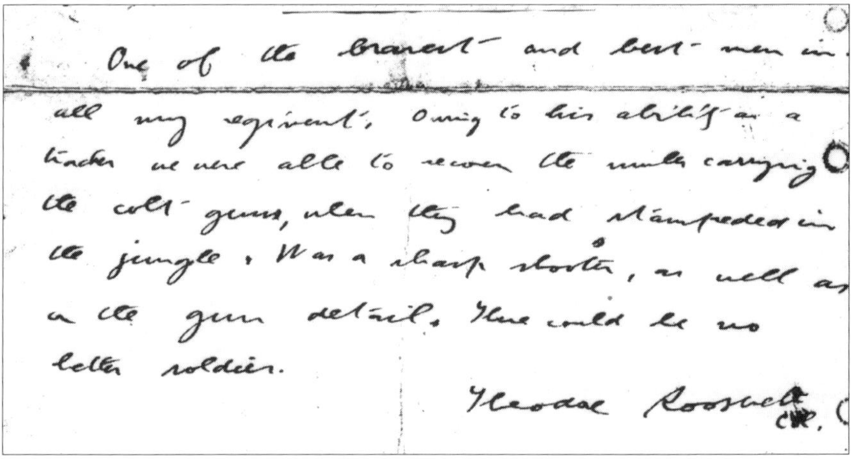

One of the bravest and best men in all my regiment. Owing to his ability as a tracker we were able to recover the mules carrying the Colt guns, when they had stampeded in the jungle. Was a sharp shooter, as well as in the gun detail. There could be no better soldier.

Theodore Roosevelt Col.

HERRIG FAMILY COLLECTION.

second lieutenant for tracking down some mules loaded with machine guns that got away during battle. He tracked the mules, after others had given up, into Spanish territory and recovered them and the guns.

When the war was over and his regiment was mustered-out, Fred said "It was more fun hunting with Roosevelt in the Dakota badlands then it was hunting with Roosevelt in Cuba." Across Fred's discharge papers Roosevelt wrote, "One of the bravest and best men in all my regiments. Owing to his ability as a tracker, we were able to recover the mules carrying the Colt guns, after they had stampeded into the jungle.

Copy

STATE OF NEW YORK
EXECUTIVE CHAMBER
ALBANY

Dec. 20th, 1899.

Hon. Thomas H. Carter,

Senate Chamber, Washington, D.C.

My dear Senator:--

The enclosed letter explains itself. It is from one of the best men in my regiment, whom I also employed on my ranch at once time. He is as honest, faithful, brave and loyal a fellow as ever walked the earth, and I have tested him thoroughly both in civil and military duties. There is no position of trust to which I should not be delighted to see him appointed if it was in his line.

Faithfully yours,

Theodore Roosevelt

HERRIG FAMILY COLLECTION.

STATE OF NEW YORK
EXECUTIVE CHAMBER
ALBANY

Dec. 20th, 1899.

Mr. Fredk. Herrig,

Kalispell, Montana.

My dear Fred:--

I will write to Senator Carter at once and back you in every way. I only hope that he will pay attention to what I say. I enclose copy of my letter.

Faithfully yours,

Theodore Roosevelt

HERRIG FAMILY COLLECTION.

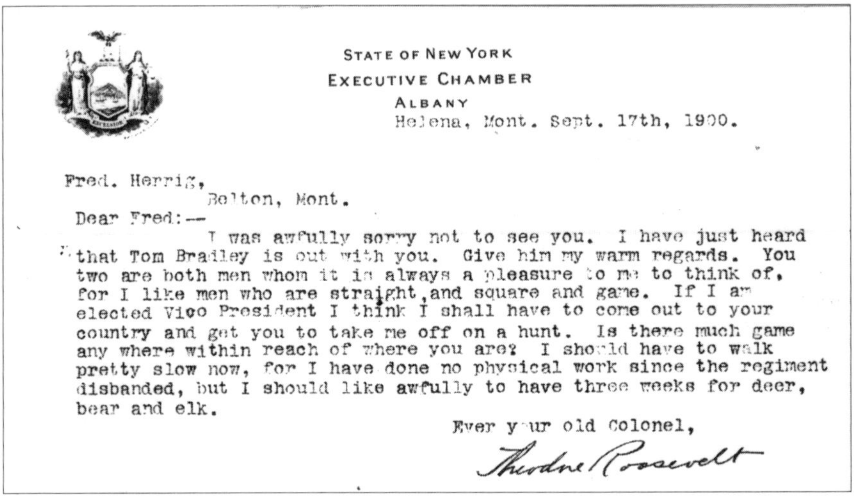

STATE OF NEW YORK
EXECUTIVE CHAMBER
ALBANY
Helena, Mont. Sept. 17th, 1900.

Fred. Herrig,
Belton, Mont.

Dear Fred:--

I was awfully sorry not to see you. I have just heard that Tom Bradley is out with you. Give him my warm regards. You two are both men whom it is always a pleasure to me to think of, for I like men who are straight, and square and game. If I am elected Vice President I think I shall have to come out to your country and get you to take me off on a hunt. Is there much game any where within reach of where you are? I should have to walk pretty slow now, for I have done no physical work since the regiment disbanded, but I should like awfully to have three weeks for deer, bear and elk.

Ever your old Colonel,
Theodore Roosevelt

HERRIG FAMILY COLLECTION.

Was a sharp shooter, as well as on the gun detail. There could be no better soldier."

Fred returned to Montana and was trying to decide what new adventure he would like to tackle when he heard about a range rider's job that had been established by the new chief of forestry. Fred, not one to go the long way when a short-cut would do, wrote to his friend Theodore Roosevelt, who was then governor of New York, and asked for a recommendation.

Fred was appointed range rider of the Upper North Fork of the Flathead Forest Reserve in 1900. His district included everything west of the North Fork of the Flathead River to the Whitefish Divide. His own district was vast, but he was asked to keep an eye on the country east of the river until a range rider was assigned to that area. Sometimes he patrolled the area east of the river to check on the happenings at the oil boom site at Kintla and the mining around Altyn. His reserve station was at Moran, but he picked up his mail in Belton.

He often heard from Roosevelt, who had an abiding interest in the character of the men and women of the west and particularly high regard for the men of his old regiment.

Frank Liebig met Fred while he was surveying mining claims near Herrig's patrol area. Frank still had a thick accent and Fred instantly recognized him as German, probably Prussian. Conversation between the Alsatian and the German started out uneasy. There were a few episodes of verbal sparring until it was plain that neither of them had any interest in what happened in Europe. Both men considered themselves Americans and neither had any interest in politics of any kind. They settled into a comfortable friendship and often passed the time swapping stories about their strikingly similar youths in the German Empire and their buckaroo days in the badlands. Fred, the more talkative of the two men, spent many hours entertaining Frank and anyone else who happened to be standing around with stories of his adventures as a trapper, a wrangler, and a Rough Rider.

Frank described Herrig as an imposing figure.

> *He was a big man, not extra tall, but broad, with powerful shoulders. He generally rode a dark bay horse, decked up with a silver-studded bridle and martingale. He wore mostly high-top boots, a big 44 strapped on his belt and he carried a 45-70 rifle in a scabbard on his saddle. He wore the ranger's badge always in plain sight, and Bruno, a big Russian wolfhound, was his steady companion.*

One day in late June 1901, Frank was coming into Belton from a trip to the Upper North Fork. Fred Herrig was hanging around, talking to some settlers. His horse was tied to a tree and Bruno lay in the shade close by. Fred looked a little down in the mouth, a sight Frank had never seen before. Frank went up to him and they exchanged pleasantries.

The Vice President's Chamber
WASHINGTON, D.C.

Oyster Bay, N.YJune 13th, 1901.

Mr. Fred. Herrig,

Kalispel, Mont.

Dear Fred:--

I have your letter of the 8th inst. I shall write to Senator Carter at once and find out if I can be of assistance.

Faithfully yours,

Theodore Roosevelt

HERRIG FAMILY COLLECTION.

The Vice President's Chamber
WASHINGTON, D.C.

Oyster Bay, N.Y, June 22nd, 1901.

Mr. Fred Herrig,

Kalispel, Montana

My dear Fred:--

The inclosed letter from Senator Carter explains itself. I am very much pleased.

Sincerely yours,

Theodore Roosevelt

HERRIG FAMILY COLLECTION.

"You take da day off, Fred?" The ranger's badge that Herrig always wore in plain sight was missing.

"More'n the day. The government tied a can to my tail over a little drinkin' party." Fred did not give any details about the little drinkin' party other than to indicate he didn't think it was anything the government ought to get excited about and sure not enough to fire him over. "I think I got the situation straightened out. They hum a different tune when they find out you're a friend of the vice president. I'll know in a few days. Right now, I'm headed north to do a little fishing."

Fred had written to Theodore Roosevelt about his predicament, and the vice president helped out his old friend.

It was late July when Fred Herrig rode over to Frank's cabin on Lake McDonald and hailed him to come out. The ranger's badge sparkled on his chest and Herrig's naturally broad, mischievous smile greeted him from atop his horse. Frank fixed them some supper and they whiled away the evening talking about Roosevelt, Fred's reinstatement as a range rider, the Forest Bureau, and the changing times.

Frank Liebig, Forest Ranger, Glacier district

By 1902, Theodore Roosevelt had been president long enough to persuade Congress to give more power and money to preserve the wilderness, and Chief Forester Gifford Pinchot was making some changes. Range riders were designated as rangers. In addition to enforcing the laws, fighting fires, and keeping the trails open, Pinchot wanted his forest officials (rangers and foresters) to be capable of surveying, estimating, and scaling timber, lumbering, and to know something about forestry and the livestock business.

Supervisor Haines needed a ranger for the Glacier District east of the Flathead River to the Blackfeet Indian Reservation. It was prime wilderness country, and there was growing interest and activity in that area. He had a good man in Fred Herrig who worked hard as a lawman of the forest and kept an eye on the Glacier country, but Fred was already assigned the huge district of the Upper North Fork, and he was not trained in forestry. Haines sent out word that he was looking for men of the sort that Gifford Pinchot wanted hired, and he expected they would not be easy to find. Fred Herrig told Haines his troubles were over—there was just such a man living at the foot of Lake McDonald.

F. N. Haines sat on a fallen log near the shore of Lake McDonald. He had been waiting there a good spell. Frank Liebig pulled his canoe onto shore eyeing Haines without comment. He had been in the Belly River country surveying his oil claims. Haines walked toward him extending his hand. "I'm looking for a good man to work as a ranger for Uncle Sam. I've heard a lot about you Mr. Liebig. I hear you don't drink or get on a spree, but the main thing is you, know this country and are not afraid of anything."

Frank tipped his hat back. He had close-set brown eyes, a straight nose, and a thick mustache curving down around his mouth. His face was lean. His hair was brown and unruly, sometimes creased into submission by the press of his hat. He tended to keep a straight, serious face, but humor flickered in his eyes and in the slight curve of his mouth.

"Would you like to tackle the job? It pays sixty a month. You board yourself and furnish your own horses."

"I make twice that with my oil claims."

"Yea, but later on there would be promotions and higher pay if you stay with the Bureau. You'll be better off in the long haul."

Frank lifted his knapsack, his fishing gear, and his rifle from the canoe. It wasn't much salary but a chance to be paid to see the wide-open spaces in all their glory. "I'll give it a try."

The two of them went to the ranger's headquarters in Kalispell where Frank completed his citizenship papers, renouncing his allegiance to Emperor Wilhelm II, which did not trouble him in the least. He filled out several Bureau of Forestry forms, nearly two feet long, and sent the whole works to the Department of the Interior in Washington, D.C.

Frank returned to Lake McDonald. He forgot about the ranger job and took a trip up the North Fork and the east side of the Rockies. It was April, still cold, but spring was on the way. He got back to Lake McDonald in June. A letter was waiting at the post office in Belton announcing he had been a Forest Ranger since May and telling him to go to Kalispell to take the oath of office and get instructions.

Frank took the train out of Belton to Kalispell. Supervisor Haines had a small one-room office upstairs in the Whipps Building. The office contained two chairs, one small table, and one wooden box containing all the official correspondence. Frank took the oath of office before a notary public. Then Haines handed him a notebook, a silver badge, a double-bitted axe, a one-man crosscut saw, a box of ammunition for his 45-70 rifle, and two big sheets of paper on which he was to write what he did each day and then send them in at the end of the month.

Frank's assignment from Haines consisted of three sentences:

> *The whole country is yours, from Belton to Canada and across the Rockies to the prairie between Waterton Lake and the foot of St. Mary Lake. You're to look for fires, timber thieves, squatters, and game violators. Go to it and good luck.*

Frank left the Whipps building and headed across town to the livery. The liveryman told him about a rancher near Columbia Falls who might be willing to sell him some horses at a reasonable price. He took the train to Columbia Falls and walked the ten miles or so to a cattle ranch that was selling off some of its horses. After a short parley, in which the rancher seemed to have gotten the best of the deal, Frank reached deep into his pocket and bought a saddle horse and two pack horses and headed out across the mountains to Lake McDonald.

He abandoned the cabin he had built at the foot of the lake and built another at the head of the lake at the base of Stanton Mountain and added some corrals for the horses. The cabin was designated a forestry station and shortly had the flag of the U.S. Bureau of Forestry flying from its rooftop. Then he began his "go-to-it-and-good-luck" job of patrolling a half million acres, with very few trails, of the area now known as Glacier National Park.

In 1892, shortly after the Great Northern Railroad laid track from Cut Bank, Montana, westward to the Flathead Valley, a small settlement sprung up around Lake McDonald. Milo Apgar, Charlie Howe, and Frank Geduhn were the first to come and settle near the lake. Milo built his cabin near the south shore at the foot of the Lake. Charlie

Flathead Forest Reserve Station, Lake McDonald.
Photograph by Frank Liebig. LIEBIG COLLECTION.

built his cabin not too far away. Frank Geduhn set up his camp there also then later moved to the head of the lake. Other early settlers—Denny Comeau, George Snyder, and Frank Kelly—also built cabins at the head of the lake. These neighbors lived a respectable distance from each other. The homesteads were dotted around the lake, sheltered by ramparts of tall cedar, pine, and fir and only the plumes of smoke from their cabin stoves, drifting upward through the thick stands of trees, marked their existence.

These early settlers had a hard time of it. They homesteaded on land more breathtakingly beautiful than the mind could imagine, but it could not be tilled into a worthwhile farm. They hunted for food and trapped for furs, and a few took jobs around Columbia Falls and Demersville to keep their homesteads going. Then Milo Apgar's enterprising wife got the bright notion of catering to the tourists who got off the train at Belton to see McDonald Lake. Tourism was picking up, encouraged by the publicity in the East created by Dr. Lyman Sperry's exploration of the glacier country and the promotion of beautiful Lake McDonald as a tourist site by F. I. Whitney, the Great Northern Railroad's passenger agent. Mrs. Apgar cooked and served meals and made money off the hungry and often wealthy tourists, a venture that caught on. Charlie Howe built guest cabins at the foot of the lake near the Apgar's to accommodate the tourists. Within a few years, Frank Geduhn had built guest cabins near the head of the lake, and George Snyder built the Snyder Hotel and launched a steamer on Lake McDonald to provide transportation for guests from the foot of the lake to his hotel.

By 1900, settlers and investors were coming in great numbers to take advantage of this rich field of free resources. Many were European immigrants who had known the severely rationed effects of their nations' overuse of the forest resources throughout the years, but they and their descendants forgot. They were gloriously intoxicated by the bonanza of timber, minerals, and game in these mountains, which were there for the taking. They helped themselves to timber, wherever it was the handiest, tore up the earth in search of gold, copper, and oil, hired professional hunters to supply their construction crews with venison and elk, and paid trappers to provide furs for the Easterners. They were, as seems to be the nature of man, conquering new territory, expanding the progress of civilization, creating and building, and on a sure path to wealth. Quite naturally, the railroad men, stockmen, lumbermen, trappers, hunters, miners, settlers, investors, and many a politician were not happy about the government's forest reserves. The 1897 Proclamation to establish the reserves had been an aggravation but had not slowed the settlers down. But when Roosevelt and Pinchot put some teeth into the reserve restrictions and men on the job to enforce them, it was a knee in their belly. Reserves held them down, cramped their private ambitions, and a ranger who had the unmitigated gall to enforce the reserve restrictions was a "yellow dog."

Frank was on good terms with the wilderness. He was an expert tracker and a crack shot with a rifle, and he was tough enough. He could outwalk some horses, and he never tired of strenuous work. He knew something about forestry. He was plainly fit for this "go-to-it" job, *with one hitch.* He was not a man to meddle in other folks' affairs. The ranger's badge meant he had to take an interest in what everyone was doing within the boundaries, lest they forget the purpose of the reserve. This part of the job would never be to his liking. He had come to America to enjoy the wide-open freedoms of the American West, and now he had a part to play in limiting the freedoms he so cherished.

But Frank had accepted the job, and like the other honest men of his time, a job was a trust to be honored without compromise. President Roosevelt and F. N. Haines wanted the Forest Reserve restrictions enforced, and whether the restrictions were fair or foul, Frank Liebig set out to see that they were obeyed.

His job was to stop the killing of game out of limits and out of season, stop the cutting of green timber, and ensure that only legally designated timber was cut. He was to prevent any further cutting of the beautiful cedar that grew around Lake McDonald and to look out for and stop mining and logging trespassing and prevent careless settlers and tourists from starting fires. There were no telephones, no roads, no ways to communicate except by a long walk or on horseback. Frank's job would be easier if he had the cooperation of the permanent settlers. He had been well liked when he was one of them, but many turned on him when he became Ranger Liebig, intent on enforcing the reserve restrictions. Some forty years later, Frank wrote:

> *I sure had my hand's full, and then some. A ranger and some mounted police were on the same footing. People always liked us a long ways off. More than once I have been waylaid, but like the preacher and the bear, the Lord was on my side. My reputation as a good shot or Uncle's badge buffaloed the trespasser, and I always came out on top.*

Frank had a vast, spectacular but punishing land to patrol and he had to be quick and regular about it. Walking through the deep, forested valleys and along the glacier-gnawed rocky ridges and climbing the proud, mighty peaks for the sheer glory of it was one thing. Patrolling for squatters, timber thieves, game poachers, and fires was a whole other matter, and it took the leisure out of a walk in the woods. He widened the old Indian and trapper pathways to get his saddle and pack horses through quickly to fight fires or chase out game and timber poachers. He widened the often-used trails from old mining camps toward the settlements for the settlers and tourists, and he cut out new trails from Lake McDonald to the Canadian border, west to the North Fork of the Flathead River and east to the Blackfeet Reservation. And for the next eight years he kept these 200 miles of old pathways and trails clear of landslides and windfalls with a crosscut saw and an axe. When the situation was impossible by axe and saw, he threw in a charge of dynamite. He patched up abandoned miner's shacks in the high country to use for shelter when he was on winter patrol for poachers and lost settlers and kept these "snowshoe" cabins stocked with firewood and food.

Frank began his regular patrols from the cabin on Lake McDonald. He awoke and rose when the black blanket of pre-dawn still covered the mountains. He breakfasted on bear meat strips, biscuits, and buttermilk then headed out on foot, carrying a palouser for light. He climbed up Stanton Mountain as dawn was breaking and waited at the top until

Hauling logs by sleigh. LIEBIG COLLECTION.

On the Camas Trail. LIEBIG COLLECTION.

the sun splashed its light across the mountains and valleys. He looked around, trying to spot the smoke from any fires that may have erupted or the billowing dust from some outlaw timbering or mining activity. Then he came back down, saddled his horse, and packed up the mule and pack horses with the tools and provisions he needed to clear trails, patrol his district, and, if need be, fight fires.

If Frank had spotted something from his climb up the mountain, he went directly there. If not, he headed out on general patrol, riding quietly through the battalions of cedar and fir northward along the North Fork of the Flathead River toward the Canadian boundary. On

Frank Liebig on his horse. LIEBIG COLLECTION.

the way, he took a look up and down Camas, Dutch, Logging, and Quartz Creeks where a few diehard prospectors still panned for gold. He checked on their welfare, shared a cup of their coffee, and looked around to see if any new enterprising mining or timber operations were being illegally set up, then he rode on. He made a patrol pass through the thick forests and shrubs around Bowman Lake, keeping a sharp eye out for disapproving grizzlies that watched him set up camp near the lakeshore. He dined on fresh-caught cutthroat trout, sizzled hot and flaky over a campfire, and washed down beans and hard bread with boiled coffee. At daybreak, he rode up to Kintla Lake and checked on

Frank Liebig crossing McDonald Creek
at the head of Lake McDonald. LIEBIG COLLECTION.

the nearly abandoned oil drilling operations. He moved on through the jungle of forest in the Kintla Valley and climbed up through the scree and rocks of Boulder Pass and over to Waterton Lake.

He cleared the trails as he went and stashed food and firewood in abandoned cabins along the way for the coming winter. Sometimes he went up into Canada and down the Belly River and over to Babb on the border of his district and the Blackfeet Reservation. At other times, he left Waterton Lake and went down through Waterton Valley to Flattop Mountain and east through the Swiftcurrent Valley to take a look around the mostly abandoned mines and pay a call on the remaining residents of Altyn. Then he crossed the mountains and came in to Saint Mary Lake. From Saint Mary he came back over Gunsight Pass and Sperry Glacier to the southeast shore of Lake McDonald. He varied his patrol often, trekking back and forth across the Continental Divide. In winter, terrible storms raged on the divide. Titan winds blew down trees, tumbled rocks, and blew snow into gigantic drifts. Sometimes the work of these winds imprisoned him on the trail and it took several days to cut himself out.

Frank surveyed boundaries, using an axe to clear lines, and he was his own instrument man, rod-man, chain-man, and stake artist.

Tourist party, head of Lake McDonald, 1903 or 1904.
GLACIER NATIONAL PARK ARCHIVES.

He led groups of university men on geological surveys through the country and let them have at it, while he studied what they did from a reasonable distance. He fought fires singlehandedly or with the help of whoever he could round up in the vicinity. *"Nature had a hand on things then and there were only small fires of ten to twenty acres until the time of the big fires in 1910."* More often than not there were few or no trails to the fire sites and new trails had to be cut and cleared. In his journal, Frank wrote, *"Came to a place where the Creek had been blocked up with driftwood. Worked several hours on the driftwood but it was too dangerous on account of the swift water, so I left it to use some dynamite tomorrow to blow a hole through, worked rest of day on trail cutting out trees."* The following day he wrote, *"Took some powder along and fixed up a charge and blowed a big hole in the drift wood pine and the water receded right away from the trail, fixed up another place where the Creek washed the trail out, rolling out rocks and filled up with earth again."*

Frank was a small wiry man, but Fred Herrig had taught him a thing or two about being imposing when it came to enforcing the law. In a short time, Frank's reputation as a strong force in the forest was legendary. He seemed to be everywhere—in the mountains, the woods, around the lakes, and along the streams. He appeared suddenly out of the forest mist to stop a poacher or prevent trees from being cut or ensure that a fire was put out. The perpetrator would look up and there, like an ominous phantom, holding them in a spell with his cast-iron smile and riveting eyes, was Ranger Liebig. *"I had to put the fear of God into a few, before they got too bold."* He shifted his weight in the saddle, the leather creaking with the movement, and let his right hand drop conspicuously to rest gently on the scabbard of the 45-70. He wasn't long on talk, and his thick German accent added threatening tenor rather than clarity to what he said, but they generally got the message and cleared out. A bluff was as good as a blow when it came to dealing with men trying to skirt the law and it didn't take long for the people in the region to realize that Frank had a sixth sense about what was going on in the forest and the will to enforce the Reserve restrictions. On that account he had their respect, if not their cooperation. The lumbermen, investors, developers, and poachers showed their respect for the determined ranger but were never happy to see him show up.

Frank was also quick to give settlers and visitors a hand when needed or carry a message from one settler or camp to another as he made his rounds. He told them where the good fishing holes were and where they might find their winter meat supply standing on the hoof. He shared his knowledge of what it took to survive in this wilderness and in the harsh and unpredictable weather. It took a few years, but eventually he became a welcome sight to the settlers and tourists.

THREE

"GO TO IT AND GOOD LUCK"

A RANGER'S JOURNAL

The first four to six years as a ranger brought me more excitement than the last twenty-five combined.

Frank's ranger district covered over a half-million acres of some of the roughest country in the United States. During his patrols, he carried a notebook to write down his experiences, give the number of miles traveled every day, and list the places visited and business transacted and how many miles of trails he made or cleared of windfalls. Once a month, he transferred this information to a big sheet of paper called the Monthly Report. *Sometimes I made the round trip by the end of the month to send in my report. Once in a while I was a week or two late—then would get heck for not being on time. Little did the officials in Washington know how big my district was.*

As the area became more popular for vacationers and sightseers, getting tourists out of dangerous predicaments took up more of Frank's time. He wrote an account of these adventures in a 1944 letter to the Forest Service for its historical publication *Early Days in The Forest Service*. The life and times of Frank Liebig and the first rangers

Rangers on patrol. LIEBIG COLLECTION.

are chronicled in those stories and other extracts from his journals. Frank's stories are sparsely told, as was his nature. They are reprinted here in his words. I have added some background information but chose not to tamper with his work and let your imagination take hold as mine did when I first read these simply stated accounts of his daily life as a ranger.

The Cree, Herrig, and Me Around 1902 or 1903

I guess the only time I was a little worried was once when word was brought to me by some homesteader that a bunch of Cree Indians had come across the Canadian border on the North Fork with about 10 or 12 lodges and 40 dogs and were killing all the moose and smoking the meat.

In the earliest history of the Indians, the Cree were known as fierce raiders. They were wanderers and did not have any fixed homelands.

They hunted game for their food. When game became scarce where they camped, they fought their way into the lands of other tribes. The Plains Cree eventually roamed throughout Canada and pushed southward into Montana as far as the Missouri River. In Montana in the early 1900s, the Cree Indians were still feared and loathed because of the murders of two priests and all the white men at Frog Lake, Canada, in 1885 and their raids on Montana cattle ranches in 1886, 1887, and 1888. The violence had been brought on by harsh winters and changes in the treaties, reducing the extent of Indian lands. When Montana became a state in 1889, many of the newspapers urged driving the Cree back into Canada as intolerable nuisances who constantly violated U.S. game laws and looted isolated cabins. The newspapers also suggested that the Cree were carriers of smallpox and would cause an epidemic along the northern borders. By 1896, the majority of the Cree were taken to various Canadian reserves. Little Bear and Lucky Man, who were known to be involved in the Frog Lake murders eleven years earlier, were charged and tried in Canada. The only living witness against them was the Cree wife of one of the men murdered. She did not identify them as the killers, and Little Bear and Lucky Man were released. By 1901, the Cree were back in Montana. The band that Liebig and Herrig came upon may have been that of Little Bear and Lucky Man. Lucky Man was described as a dreadful-looking rascal, thin and emaciated, with his face seamed by a thousand wrinkles.

I sent word to Ranger Herrig, stationed at Moran, to meet me at Round Prairie near Bowman Creek. I also took F. Geduhn, a homesteader from the head of Lake McDonald, and we all met at the place mentioned. Well, to make the story short, we found nine tepees north of Kintla Creek near a big willow flat. And we found plenty of meat over some poles with a fire underneath. Geduhn held my horse while I walked up to the tepees, where three or four Cree Indians were cutting up some meat. Ranger Herrig rode just fifty feet behind me, his rifle all ready for action. I had my rifle in my hands too. When we got close to the camp we were met by about twenty or more dogs. Men came from everywhere, and all the squaws and kids ran into the tepees.

I hollered for the chief to come out. Finally, a diseased-looking Indian stepped out and made himself known as the responsible party. I told him that he came across the line and not to kill any more moose. He said they had a fire across the line which drove all the moose into the United States and they were hard up for winter food. I told him again that they ran all the game out of the country with their dogs. Some of the Indians didn't want to go. I told them they had to break camp next morning or we would kill all the dogs.

The Indians could not exist without the dogs. These dogs were trained to surround a moose and hold him until the Indian comes up and kills him.

We went to their camp next day about the middle of the forenoon, and there were no signs of breaking their camp. This time Indians were hiding behind tents and trees, no squaws in sight, but plenty of dogs. The old Indian chief was there to meet me and said they couldn't move for a week yet until all their meat was cured.

First thing three or four shots crashed out, and a couple of dead dogs rolled on the ground. Ranger Herrig couldn't stand it any longer and wanted to mop up all the dogs. I got ready for action also, thinking that the Indians sure would get even with us. So, I hollered to Herrig and Geduhn to hold their fire for a minute to see what the Indians had to say. Everything was confusion in the camp, and I thought lead would be flying in our direction any second. Then the chief hollered and told me they would move immediately. The lodges went down, and in three hours they were on the trail up the North Fork and across the Canadian border. We hung around for several days, but the Crees stayed away.

Little Bear joined forces with Rocky Boy and his band of Chippewa to seek a permanent home in the United States for their followers. In 1909, their homeless and starving conditions touched the hearts of Helena residents, and a campaign was launched to provide food and to aid Little Bear and Rocky Boy in their quest for a homeland. In 1916, a permanent reservation of 56,035 acres in the Milk River country was set aside as Rocky Boy's Indian Reservation for his band of Chippewa, the Cree, and other homeless Indians in Montana.

Cold Trail to a Hot Fire

The very next year Ranger Herrig saved me from drowning. It was in October, and bitterly cold nights. Sheet ice was floating down the North Fork. Riding up the river, I saw a big smoke rising up in the Coal Creek area on the west side of the river. I rode to the head of the Big Prairie to get a couple of settlers to help me on the fire. Just before I got to the place the horse stepped in a badger hole and nearly broke his leg. He was useless for a week. When I arrived at the homesteader's place nobody was home. I put the horse in the corral to look the fire over on foot.

Before I got to the river here comes Ranger Herrig to pay me a visit. He saw the smoke also. And we decided to tackle the fire at once. We got a mattock and a couple of axes and left word for the settlers to follow when they came home. When we came to the river crossing, which was about 100 yards wide and two and half feet at the deepest place, I had to wade across the river, as his horse would not stand for a double load. So he crossed over with the horse, and the big Russian wolfhound, and myself following.

I had off my shoes and pants and underwear, to be dry when I got over. Before I got two-thirds across I got the cramps in my legs in the ice-cold water. My legs refused to move, and I had to drag myself on my hands toward the shore in about twenty inches of water. Herrig just got across, when he looked back and saw what happened. He rode the horse right back and caught me just in time and dragged me on to the shore. I lost my memory for twenty minutes and when I came to, Herrig was rubbing my body and legs to get circulation in my body started. After an hour I was in shape to hit the trail again, and we had quite a stretch of the fire surrounded when the settlers arrived. One settler had a horse which didn't mind a double load in crossing the river, and I sure made use of it. The fire was either a lightning hangover or started by hunters. I think it was the latter.

The Great Canoe Rescue

In 1903, I came across the divide from the Camas Lakes on foot and cached my canoe in the woods to cross Lake McDonald to the other side. A big swell was on the lake and four-foot waves, but not dangerous for the canoe, and I could handle it without trouble. When I got nearly across I saw a bunch of people standing on the shore with their arms stretched out as if they were pointing. I thought at first, they were watching me and the canoe disappearing in the trough of the waves, and then on the crest of the next one. It finally dawned on me that the people were pointing in another direction. I began to look around, and when I came up on top of a high wave I spotted a rowboat full of water and a man and woman hanging on to it. I worked the canoe close to the outfit to look her over. The people were pretty well chilled and nearly done for in the cold water. The woman said she could swim a little, but the man could not. When I got real close, the woman let loose of the boat and grabbed the canoe, nearly upsetting me. I had to hit her on the hands with the paddle and once over the head, partly stunning her, before she let loose and moved to the end of the canoe. It was a ticklish business to get her into the canoe without upsetting. I got hold of her hair, and watching my chances, I told her to kick hard with her feet, which she finally did, and I managed to drag her into my canoe. I also got it half full of water, and I had to bail water with a five-pound lard pail to beat the band. The woman had fainted when she got into the canoe. After I had most of the water out so that I could manage my canoe again, I went carefully up to the man and tried to give him the rope from the canoe to hang onto so that I could tow him to shore, but he was all in and would not let loose of the boat, although every other wave went over his head. I finally got the rope around under his arms and told him to keep his head above the water and started for the shore.

It didn't come out the way I had it planned, as the man rolled over in the water and was half drowned when I reached shore.

Forest Reserves Combined

In 1903, the Flathead and Lewis and Clark Reserves were combined into the Lewis and Clark Forest Reserve. The new Lewis and Clark Reserve was divided by the Great Northern Railroad into the Northern and Southern Districts, with some small changes in the boundaries of the old Flathead and Lewis and Clark Reserves. *Nothing much else changed on my end of things. Ranger Herrig was assigned to a new district west of the Whitefish Mountain Range near Fortine and T. Christenson took over the Upper North Fork.*

First Ranger's Meeting

Our first ranger meeting, if I remember right, was held at the foot of Lake McDonald in 1904, with about five or six assistant rangers helping out, a Mr. Sherman and a Mr. Clapp from Washington, D.C. visiting us, and mostly supervising the meeting, telling us there would be a great change in the Forest Bureau in the near future, which was true. The very next year the Forestry Bureau was transferred from the Department of the Interior to the Department of Agriculture.

In 1905, the Forestry Division of the General Land Office and the Bureau of Forestry combined under the Department of Agriculture to become the U.S. Forest Service.

Egan Siding

In 1904 we had a very heavy snow fall. It started snowing Oct 20 and kept up until three feet was piled up at Belton along the Great Northern Railroad. A hunting party of three men, Dr. H. Houston and his brother Rodney Houston, a dentist from Kalispell, Mr. Egan, Division Superintendent of the Great Northern Railroad went on a deer hunt four mile below Belton near Lake Five. They

hooked a special car on the train and told the conductor to side track the car at Belton, as they intended to sleep and eat in the car that evening. The party got off the train at Lake Five and the train went on to Belton. The agreement was to hunt from Lake Five towards Belton following the railroad more or less. It started to snow in the forenoon and more and more in the afternoon, so that there was about six feet of fresh snow. The Houston brothers made it to Belton by supper time--went into the special car and waited for the superintendent to show up to have supper together. He never showed up. They finally ate alone, thinking Mr. Egan killed a deer late and couldn't make it in by dark and possibly stayed over night with some homesteaders around Lake Five. Snowed hard all night and by morning a good foot of fresh snow had fallen, covering all tracks made the day before. In the morning the party waited until about 10 a.m., and as the superintendent didn't show up, they went down to Lake Five, visiting the settlers and inquiring about Mr.Egan. Nobody had seen him. Then they got alarmed and gathered a number of men together and tried to find the lost hunter. Old tracks were hard to follow and it was snowing all the time. In the afternoon, an emergency call was sent in to the headquarters at Whitefish and a car-load of men were sent by train to Lake Five. They hunted all night and no trace of the hunter.

An engine went up and down the track blowing the whistle, in order to draw the lost hunter to the railroad track. No luck—snow piling up. At that time, I was in the Camas Lake country and had a hard time making it across the hump to Lake McDonald. Here I used the boat and when I came to Belton for my mail, I heard about the lost superintendent. A reward was out. $1,000 for the person who found him, dead or alive. I organized a searching party, but gave up after two days of hunting, as the woods were full of tracks of men every place.

The rumor got around that the superintendent was shot by the Houston brothers, by mistake for a deer, and then cached under some logs.

In order to clear themselves of suspicion the man had to be found. In the first part of May we organized a searching party again and started at Lake Five and worked back and forth towards Belton. I had sixteen men in the crew. The hunt lasted ten or eleven days. We finally found the superintendent three quarters mile below Belton and a quarter mile from the railroad track. We found the man on a small knoll, laying face down—his temple on a six-foot fallen lodgepole log. His hat laid on the other side of the log. His watch had slipped out of his pocket. In his pocket, some rifle cartridges and money but no rifle or compass. These articles were never found. We didn't move the body until the coroner came. The snow was gone in the open places when we found the man and his body was in good shape except the face which had been exposed for some time. The coroner cut the clothes from his body and looked him over—could not find any broken bones and he wasn't shot either. The verdict was that the man died from heart failure or may have stumbled in the dark hitting his head on the log, as it showed that he never moved after he fell. He must of been rattled, as he had to cross three or four logging roads, all leading to the railroad track and could almost see the train in daylight. Station Five where they started the hunt that fatal day was re-named by the Great Northern and called the new Egan Siding.

Lake Five. Great Northern train in distance on the left. LIEBIG COLLECTION.

Double Crossing

The very next fall, in 1905, a railroad engineer from Whitefish went hunting three miles below Belton on a strip of timber a half mile wide between the railroad and the Middle Fork of the Flathead River. He was with a friend and they were figuring on staying in the Belton Hotel for a few days. The engineer didn't show up that night. I happened to be at the foot of Lake McDonald that night and received word to come and find the man. I went to Belton and early the next morning I took two extra woodsmen with me—some sandwiches and a bottle of hot milk.

The man that hunted with him, showed me the place where he saw his partner the last time and I began following his tracks in the snow. The man sure had me guessing—he had followed a large deer for several hours and finally lost him. He got so rattled in his direction that he did not know which way to go. There was only one Great Northern Railroad in this part of the State and he was an engineer on a freight train, but it seems to make no difference, as he crossed the railroad tracks four times—but deliberately walked away, thinking the railroad should be across the river. I found several places where he had tried to cross the

river, but found it too deep, wide and cold. I finally found him huddled over a small fire—his face all black from the smoke—gave him my sandwiches and bottle of milk. I had an awful time explaining to him we had to follow the railroad track to Belton—he still thought I was wrong, until we came to Belton.

Fire Watch

The timber in those early days was sure marvelous. Very few fire scars—just little patches from one to twenty acres—until 1910, when we had the real big fires ever since.

Oct 18, 1905, was visited by Supt. Haines and Kotch again on trail work. In the notebook, I mentioned to them about climbing Mt. Stanton, which gave me a good view over a good part of my district. I mentioned this because they made fun of me climbing mountain peaks to look for fires. They thought it was too much work and would wait until the fire got good and big, so they could see it easily. (In 1910, Frank presented his ideas on fire patrol at a rangers meeting.) *Little did I dream that 25 years later, lookouts would be stationed on such high points.*

Aug 8,1906—I climbed to the top of Stanton Mountain at the head of Lake McDonald, to have a look at the surrounding country and discovered smoke rolling up across a small mountain range in the Little Saint Mary's Creek, which proved to be, in a

Right: Bill Daughs, Forest Guard, Fish Creek Cabin, Lake McDonald.
GLACIER NATIONAL PARK ARCHIVES.

Left: A ranger on patrol.
LIEBIG COLLECTION.

day or two, my first large lightning fire; about 70 acres. I had to blaze a trail to the fire, from the nearest trail, and got men from Belton and firefighting equipment. Half of our transportation had to be done by row-boat and the rest packed in on our back. This took several extra days. No telephones in my district as yet.

A man by the name of B. Daughs started at Lake McDonald as a guard, helped me in the early days of 1904–06 on trail work. We were working at one time on the Continental Divide near the headwaters of the Belly River and Mineral Creek when we spotted a big smoke in the North Fork Valley between Quartz and Bowman Creek, so we cut across country, below Vulture Peak and down Logging Creek and Lake. The shortest distance not over twenty miles, but what a country. We made it but that was all. Horses nearly all in, and ourselves too. Not much clothes left on us either. Half the time a trapper's trail and the other half a mountain goat's trail. And when we finally got to the fire a thunderstorm came up. Lord, how it rained, and how cold we were. We didn't say much, but we thought a lot—nothing pleasant either.

Lady of the Glacier

In 1905 or 1906, I made a round trip across the Rockies and back via Flattop Mountain and down to Waterton Lake, where the million-dollar Prince of Wales Hotel is now. At that time there was only a dim trapper's trail to follow up and a trapper's hut to

Sperry Glacier. PHOTOGRAPH BY FRANK LIEBIG. LIEBIG COLLECTION.

stay in overnight; but as a rule, I preferred to stay in my small tent, which I always carried on my pack horse. On these trips I stayed quite often overnight with the Mounties in the barracks at Pincerton. These redcoats were sure a fine class of men and helped me out on several occasions, one time even putting out a small fire for me. I was treated like I belonged to them, and they were much interested in our affairs. I used to stock up with grub at a store in Mountain View, a Mormon settlement near the Belly River, and always found one or two redcoats hanging around.

One overnight stopping place used to be at Babbs near the foot of the lower Saint Mary Lake and back into the good old U.S.A. Here we had a small sawmill near the lake and I had to check up on the timber and stumpage. At the narrow on upper Saint Mary, another old hut provided shelter for the night. Sometimes I stayed in the old mining town Altyn if I returned over Swift Current Pass. By Saint Mary Lake I came out over Gunsight Pass and Sperry Glacier basin and thence to Lake McDonald.

On one of these trips coming in across Gunsight Pass, I came in late one evening into Sperry Glacier basin with my horses, ready

Frank Liebig coming over Gunsight Pass. LIEBIG COLLECTION.

to set up my tent for the night. I saw a crowd of people a little ways off and heard someone saying "There is the ranger now." And soon some people came running over and said a woman had fallen into a crevasse in Sperry Glacier and they didn't know how to get her out. In the meanwhile they had sent a man down to the hotel ten miles away to get some ropes. No telephone on the Forest yet. The first telephone was installed from Belton to the hotel in 1910.

When the people told me about the woman falling into the crevasse, I turned the horses loose in a hurry and grabbed two lash ropes and the axe and told the men to "come on."

The place was a quarter of a mile to the edge of the glacier, and about 250 yards across the ice to the crevasse. I cut a stunted green fir tree four or five inches across and five feet long, and had the men pack it along. When we got to the glacier three or four men stood at the place where the woman slid in. Two women and three more men came along, with them a minister of the gospel by the name of Falls—a real mountaineer. He died in Seattle two years later. I selected a place on the lower side of the crevasse and chopped a deep hole in the ice and set the green post into the hole and packed ice all around to make it fairly solid. I tied the two lash ropes together and tied a number of knots into the rope for a

Gunsight Pass area. LIEBIG COLLECTION.

good hand hold. Then I tied the rope to the post sticking above the ice and told a couple of men to hang onto the post so it couldn't slip out and threw the rope into the crevasse.

I could see the woman lying almost horizontal in the ice. The crevasse was about four or five feet wide on the top and came together to a knife edge on the bottom, about 35 feet down. She was wedged in at about 30 feet, and dead as a door nail. I slid down the rope, and had some sweat worked up, and when I got down into the crevasse was it cold! I tried to hang onto the rope and pull the woman loose but couldn't budge her. We thought she was dead anyway, so I stepped on her body to rest my feet and told the men to haul up the rope and send the axe down, which they did. Then I chopped a hole on each side of the ice big enough to put my feet in for a hold, then sent the axe up again to the top. When the rope came down again I started to pull the woman loose, and nearly pulled her arm out she was wedged in so tight. But I finally got her loose and managed to get the rope around her waist and the men pulled her up to the surface and then let the rope down again.

I was so frozen by this time I was in doubt that I could climb the rope so I put it under my arms and was hauled out

A crevasse in Sperry Glacier. Photograph by Norman A. Forsyth.
LIBRARY OF CONGRESS, LC-DIG-STEREO-1S13711.

by the men too. When I got out I could hardly stand up I was so cold and had to stamp around a bit to get my blood in circulation again.

We had plenty of help by this time. Someone brought a lantern and candles from the camp as it was getting dark. There was no stretcher so four men got hold of the woman, one on each leg and one on each arm, and one man went ahead with the lantern. When we got to the edge of the ice there was a narrow trail leading down through the rocks and around some cliffs, one cliff over twenty feet high. We thought it would be safer for all of us to let the body down on our rope over the cliff. Someone went ahead to receive the body below. They had a palouser going and we could see the light below. When the body was half-way

down, the woman began to spin around and hit her head on the rocks, cutting quite a gash, which must have brought her to her senses because she let out an awful yell. Her terrible yell scared us half to death as we had all thought she was a goner for sure. Then she fainted again.

We finally got her to the camp where they had a big fire going and lots of hot coffee and lots more of hot drinks, and we all had our share of the hot brandy. Even the minister of the gospel and yours truly, even if I was on the water wagon. I had my share and don't know today how I got into my sleeping bag only half undressed I think someone else must have helped me.

A doctor came up towards morning and pronounced the woman O.K. Some men and women filled her up all night with hot brandy until she was glorious drunk. We sure had a late breakfast next day.

Regular Blizzard

I think it was late in the fall of 1907 when I received a letter from the Supervisor to meet Chief Forester Pinchot and a party from Washington D.C. at Swift Current Pass to take them down to Lake McDonald and thence to Belton. (President Roosevelt had enlarged the Reserve again, and the officials from Washington were on a familiarization tour after hearing complaints from the administrative people that the Reserve was already too big to handle.) *It was a two-day trip from the head of the lake to Granite Park where I had an old mining cabin which was ready to fall in.*

Here was good horse feed. From the cabin it was about two miles to the pass. During the night the weather changed and by noon a regular blizzard was raging. Nevertheless, I hit the pass by noon and hung around there for several hours. Then I finally gave up, intending to go back to the miner's cabin.

I knew the party never could make it over the pass in such a storm. When I turned back I couldn't see 25 feet ahead. The horse trail was obliterated by the snow and everything looked alike to me, and the horses refused to go ahead. The storm was getting worse. I had to get off the saddle horse and lead both of them. I was floundering for over an hour in the snow when I realized I was lost. I found a clump of scrubby whitebark pine and got into some shelter.

Here the horses quit altogether and turned their heads with the wind. I wanted to go alone to hunt for the cabin but was afraid I couldn't find my horses again. I stuck it out for an hour

trying to figure out where I was. It was an area only two square miles but in a snowstorm like this a quarter mile is plenty big enough. I finally dragged the horses after me again, and by good fortune, hit a patch of heavy timber that looked rather familiar to me. I left the horses and began to scout around. I found a blaze on a tree and discovered I was in the trail. I hit the old cabin in fifteen minutes. I went back at once and got the horses and gave them a feed of oats in a sheltered place behind the cabin. And how that storm raged all night! Three feet of snow in the morning, and the blizzard stayed another day. I had to go half a mile before I left Granite Park to get down into the valley. It took me one hour to make that half mile. By noon I was on the bottom of the valley and found only one foot of snow and hardly any wind, but you could hear the storm still raging around the peaks.

A week later I received a letter stating that the party gave up the trip across the Continental Divide after they got as far as to the foot of Swift Current. The miners advised the party that it wouldn't be safe. A good thing they took the hint.

More than two dozen horses lost their lives over the cliffs and one person was killed while I was ranger over that Continental Divide district. And all these worries could have been avoided if we had had a telephone in those days.

More Boundary Changes

In 1908 the 1903 version of the Lewis and Clark Reserve was divided into two national forests. The Northern District, which was the old Flathead Forest Reserve became the Blackfeet National Forest. The Southern District which included most of the old Lewis and Clark Reserve became the Flathead National Forest. None of these changes had much effect on my job except to require more boundary surveys.

(In 1935, the Blackfeet National Forest was divided between the Flathead National Forest and the Kootenai National Forest.)

Help At Last

In the summer of 1908 the Government was kind to me, as they gave me a man to help on trail work as well as in fire patrol work in a place where they now (1940s) have about four to five trail crews, four lookouts and three guards. It was a blessing I had the extra man in 1908 as we had many lightning storms and tourists were coming in thick and fast; also, careless campers and smokers. It kept us hopping, putting out small fires.

Lake McDonald was beginning to get famous, as many applications began to come in for building lots for summer homes and also small timber sales—mostly cedar home logs. A small 25 ft gas boat operated by Frank Kelly sailed between the foot and head of the Lake carrying passengers and supplies for the Hotels. In the contract to run the boat on government waters, a clause was inserted to carry Forest officials free of charge if they were on official duty. I sure made use of this clause, as I could see both slopes of the mountains from the middle of the Lake when watching for fires.

In the fall of 1908, J. E. Lewis, which then owned the Glacier Hotel near the head of Lake McDonald, installed the first telephone to the hotel—the line following the trail on the east shore of the Lake. The government telephone lines in this district were installed after the Park was created in July 1910. This was the year when we had such large fires all over Western Montana and Idaho.

Full-Fledged Ranger Meeting

I have one more item I would like to mention. Our regular full-fledged ranger meeting was held on April 4, 1910, at the Point of Rocks Ranger Station near Olney, Montana on the Blackfeet National Forest. I still have the photograph in my album, and I prize it highly. I don't know who has the film. I have all the names of the men and the Supervisor and Mr. Silcox, at that time District Forester. Mr. Silcox, with his derby hat, looks more like a lawyer than a forester.

Supervisor Haines, Rangers Bruce, Cox, Joe Cosley, and Liebig on shoulder of Chief Mountain, 1907. PHOTOGRAPH BY FRANK LIEBIG. LIEBIG COLLECTION.

Rangers' meeting, Point of Rocks Ranger Station, Olney, Montana, April 10, 1910. Standing (left to right): Brunner, Frank Liebig, Joe Cosley, Christensen, Wise, Woesner, Eastland, Taylor, and Forester Silcox. Seated (left to right): Fred Herrig, Owens, Clark, DeGroot, and Supervisor Haines. U.S. FOREST SERVICE PHOTOGRAPH. LIEBIG COLLECTION.

Notes from my journal. Mon. April 4, 1910. Went with Supervisor F. N. Haines and Guard Clark on noon train to Olney for a Ranger meeting. Got there about supper time and found most of the rangers there already.

April 5, 1910. We had a Ranger meeting on Point of Rocks Ranger Station, near Olney. Attended the meeting all day. Topics of the day were: Patrol ways, Lookouts and stations, which was given by myself. Then we had a discussion of the free use system.

FOUR

GRIZZLIES AND GOATS

> Everybody can't be a Frank Liebig. Mr. Liebig of Kalispell, Montana has long been an object of awe and curiosity in his community as a result of his whacking down a monster silver-tip grizzly with one measly little pellet from a .22 rifle. And a single shot rifle, at that, if you please. (Harry M. Forwood writing in *Esquire Magazine*, July 1936, "Better Try the Neck.")

Frank had settled his status in the wild when he first came to the American wilderness. He was neither ruler nor subject. He respected the domain of the wilderness monarchs, but he would not be pushed around by fang or claw. He, just as they, kept his belly fed with the meat of wild animals, the fish of the waters, and the herbs and berries of the wilderness. Some prime country he never hunted, leaving it to the rule of the grizzly and as the dinner plate of the wolf and the mountain lion. Other areas were just naturally the hunting grounds for all God's creatures, including himself. But the grounds around his cabin and the Forest Service camps were his own sovereignty, and he declared them off-limits to bears, mountain lions, wolves, and coyotes. *Bear was my main diet as I had to declare war on these animals as they broke into camps very often and destroyed my grub.*

Frank carried a .45-70 in the scabbard on his saddle as a handy warning to timber thieves and game poachers and as a reachable weapon for mean-spirited grizzlies and outlaw lions. But when he was walking around in the wilderness he usually carried a single-shot .22.

> Men who have hunted grizzlies will say that a grizzly can take more lead and keep coming than any other animal on the North American continent. Instances have been related of grizzlies that kept roaring on toward hunters while his head, legs, and body were being blasted apart by projectiles from high-powered rifles. Other instances have been recorded where the largest of grizzlies was put down to stay with one shot. However, the weapon of destruction was considerably larger than a .22 rifle. Frank was with a party of timber cruisers working on the Middle Fork of the Flathead River near the south boundary of the present-day Glacier Park.
>
> Suddenly, a large grizzly appeared and stood up on its hind feet in the peculiar manner characteristic of bears. Without thinking, Frank raised his .22 rifle and let drive. The small piece of lead punctured the bear just below the ear and the bear fell to the ground, quivered, and lay still.
>
> In telling of the incident which Frank was reluctant to do, he said, "I just didn't stop to think. When I realized how foolish I had been, I broke out in a cold sweat. I never should have done such a foolish thing." Years later Frank still called himself some fancy names because of his actions that day. (From *The Spokesman Review*, Oct 28, 1956, "Tales from The Long Ago".)

Obviously, Frank had learned something that day about hunting grizzlies with a .22. C. S. Webb, a forest ranger, relates this story in Volume 2 of *Early Days in the Forest Service.*

> In 1919, and for some years before, the Kalispell Lumber Company operated a band mill by the railroad on Dickey Creek. They decked logs on Dickey Creek and by use of splash dams,

Frank Liebig's grizzly bear. PHOTOGRAPH BY FRANK LIEBIG. LIEBIG COLLECTION.

Rangers' horses grazing on Flattop Mountain.
PHOTOGRAPH BY FRANK LIEBIG. LIEBIG COLLECTION.

Rangers on a pack trip near Chief Mountain.
PHOTOGRAPH BY FRANK LIEBIG. LIEBIG COLLECTION.

drove the logs down this small creek to their mill. Frank Liebig was in charge of this sale. He had a few large decks to scale that fall, and I went along one morning to assist him. Previously, Frank set a medium-sized bear trap under one of the log piles, expecting to get a small black bear which had been hanging around there. He hadn't told me of the trap, but he was carrying a small single-shot .22 rifle. As we came up fairly close to the log deck, a large grizzly came rearing and screaming out from under the deck. The trap was holding the bear but didn't appear too secure. Frank pulled up his gun. I said, "Don't shoot him with that thing, Frank, if the trap doesn't hold, he will get you." But Frank pulled the trigger and the grizzly dropped stone dead. Frank had done that before, knew the exact spot in the ear to place his shot and that was what he did.

Jud and the Bear

In Frank's time, grizzlies were abundant in Glacier, and he often mentioned the number of grizzly bears he had seen on the north side of Flattop Mountain. Three of his friends, Sharp, Obrion, and Hill, who he had fished and hunted with several times, asked Frank to guide them. They had a string of seven pack horses besides their own mounts and planned to stay several days. It was a two-day trip each way, and the time of the year made heavy blankets a necessity. They were careful about not taking unnecessary stuff, but each horse had a good load going up.

On the afternoon of the second day, they were nearing the summit of Flattop. They left their duffels in a stand of firs where there was plenty of water and a sheltered place to set up their camp. Then they went on to the north side of the mountain. They looked over the ridge into a meadow on the north slope and saw five bears digging for gophers or mice in the meadow. They were upwind and the hike to come up on the downwind side of the bears was going to be long and hard. Jud Obrion had been feeling ill all day and asked to be excused. He said he would keep the horses while the other three men went after the bears.

Jud took the lead rope and tied it around his waist and sat down. He leaned his head against a rock. The sun warmed him. He grew drowsy and fell into a deep sleep. The horses, still tied into the pack string and the pack string tied to Jud, pawed through the thin layer of snow and lazily grazed the sparse grasses. Jud slept so soundly that he had no idea of time nor how his partners were making out on their hunt. He didn't hear any of the shooting that took place.

Sharp, Hill, and Frank made the long climb around the ridge and came up within about eighty yards of the grizzlies. They stepped around a large boulder and fired. The closest bear fell with the first volley. The biggest grizzly, a silver tip, bit at his shoulder, let out a cry of pain, and took off in a fast lumbering run toward the pass where Jud was watching the horses. All the lead that they could throw at the fleeing bear did not slow him down as he climbed the steep pitch. When he gained the level part of the ridge, he made even faster time.

The first Jud knew of any disturbance was when he was jerked out of his senses by the lead rope. The horses pulled him along the ground and piled themselves up in a heap as they fell over their ropes in an effort to escape the bear. The big silver tip had no plans to detour off the trail. He came directly through the pack string, blowing a bloody froth into Jud's face as he passed, and picked up speed going down the trail. Jud's horse and two or three others were down. The others had broken their ropes and made their getaway down the trail. Jud's rifle was in the scabbard on the downed horse. Legs and hooves were flying in every direction and Jud was having a tough time getting his gun. By the time he did he was so excited he forgot to take the gun off the safe position. He made several pulls on the trigger before he realized he had to slip off the safety. He was shaking too much to hold a bead. By this time the bear was so far down the trail that Jud just pointed the gun in the general direction and fired.

The bear made his way down the trail with spooked horses running in front of him and the rest of the horses, unable to get themselves up, left in a tangle behind. Jud looked around at the mess. He was too sick to worry about the horses—they'd have to work it out on their own. His own legs were shaking and too weak to stand on. He plopped down with a groan and just sat there.

When Frank, Sharp, and Hill came up on the ridge, they found Jud leaning back against a rock with his head in his hands and white as the snow around him. "Ya hurt, Jud?" they asked.

Jud groaned and finally got his words out. "Hell no, but I'll never be the same again."

Frank and Sharp gathered up the runaway horses while Hill helped Jud make it over to their campsite with four of the horses and their packs. The deep eerie darkness of mountain nights had settled over the camp by the time the horses were rounded up and tethered nearby and the four men were gathered around the campfire. Sharp was elected camp cook

and was squatted down next to the campfire turning strips of sizzling meat in a skillet over the fire. Frank was lacing together a broken pack strap and softly whistling a tune. Jud felt a little better and sat quietly in the glow of the fire's warmth. Hill finished up staking his tent.

"Hear that griz' spit right in your face 'fore he moseyed on down the trail, Jud!" Sharp held a straight face, never taking his eyes off the skillet.

"Hill, you talk to dang much!" Jud had told Hill the whole story while Frank and Sharp were rounding up the horses. "The danged bear was running like hell and big as this stinkin' mountain."

"Mighty disrespectful bear!" Frank said as he snapped the repaired leather strap, testing its strength.

"A man oughtn't put up with a thing like that, no sir-ree!" Sharp mumbled aloud, as he scooted the meat around the pan with a long fork then stirred the pot of beans sitting on a hot rock on the edge of the fire.

"Take it easy on Jud. He's been feelin' poorly." Hill stepped up to the fire, rubbed his hands over the flame to warm them then turned his backsides to the heat. "Course the griz' had 'um in a pre-dic-ament. Horse upside down, rifle on the underneath. I'd say that bear took advantage of ya, Jud."

Jud reddened until he might ignite. He pushed himself up and crawled into his tent. "I ain't hungry. See you jackasses tomorrow."

Frank, Sharp, and Hill erupted into spasms of laughter and didn't stop until they each had a say at every hilarious thought they could come up with about Jud and the grizzly. When they finished eating and had worn themselves out laughing they turned in for the night. Frank called out as he climbed into his tent, "I saw some goats on the rim of the mountain to the north. While we're up here, why not take home our winter supply of goat meat."

Dances with Goats

The next morning, Jud was feeling fit and ignored the chuckles of his hunting partners as they gulped down boiled coffee, chewed on the leftover meat from the night before, and busied themselves around the camp, getting ready for the goat hunt. When the duffel was stowed

A chance at a mountain goat meant a possible supply of meat for the winter.
PHOTOGRAPH BY FRANK LIEBIG. LIEBIG COLLECTION.

and the horses saddled and packed, they mounted up and rode part way up the mountain toward the meadow where Frank figured the goats would be grazing. They planned to make a sneak attack. About halfway up the mountainside, they tethered the horses and went on foot. Frank and Sharp walked around the side of the mountain and came up on the meadow from the north, while Jud and Hill climbed to the rim of the ridge to wait for the goats to be driven their way. While Jud and Hill waited for Frank and Sharp to make it around to the north side of the meadow, Jud decided to climb up on the rim of a shelf where he would have a better view of the surroundings. Hill stayed down at the bottom of the rim, in the event the goats came that way from the meadow. After an allowed amount of time, they started walking in the direction of the meadow and soon heard shooting, which meant the other men had found the goats. Hill was walking along at the bottom and Jud on the shelf of the rim. Jud had an excellent view and was expecting a goat to come bouncing along below him where it would have little chance of escaping his advantage and good shooting. He came to a corner of the shelf where it was only a few feet wide and slanted toward the edge, a drop off of 200 or 300 feet to the rocks below. He was making slow progress, his eyes on the ground, fearful of an accidental slip to his death. A big billy goat came around the corner with nothing else in mind but to escape the noise that had interrupted his morning feed in the meadow below. As Jud raised his gun to fire, his foot slipped and he fell to his knees. He froze, forgot the goat, and grabbed for a bush to check his movement toward the edge. The big billy was in a hurry and didn't like passing near the edge any more than Jud liked being there. As Jud fell to his knees, the billy jumped. He landed on Jud's head and shoulders with all four feet, shoving him down into the dirt and making him a good springboard for his next jump. It all happened so quickly that Jud could not recover to shoot the billy. He just lay there dazed.

The sad thing for Jud was that this all happened in plain sight of Hill who was at the bottom of the rim. Sharp and Frank had also come into view of the shelf and had seen it all. They were bursting with laughter at Jud's predicament and were not inclined to shoot the billy, who had produced a grand comedy for them.

The billy disappeared around the mountain. Jud heard the loud laughter below and knew he was in for more jokes. In less than two days he had been the victim of circumstance and would have to stand the fun poked at him the rest of his life. He silently climbed down the mountain, walked to his horse and went straight back to camp. When the rest of the party came in, they found Jud rolled up in his bed where he stayed until they were ready to start for home. His face was still red, and he never got over blushing when they mentioned how Jud tipped his hat to a rude grizzly and did a do-si-do with a mountain goat.

Rocky Mountain Dynamite

Frank related the following story in his 1944 letter to the Forest Service. The illustration of the incident was published in *Outdoor Life* in 1946.

I could tell lots of bear stories, but you will no doubt have lots of them from other sources. I have a story about a Rocky Mountain goat that might be of interest to you, but it was not to me.

I had always a craze to have a pet bear or deer or something around the station. In 1905 or 1906, Supervisor F. N. Haines and myself made a trip after Christmas to Avalanche Lake to see if a bridge could be built across the creek without much expense. On the head of Lake McDonald, we had about a foot of snow, but near Avalanche Lake there was about three feet and we had to use our snowshoes. When we got to the foot of the lake, we saw a bunch of mountain goats crossing on the ice, going from one shore to the other. The goats had a regular trail through the deep snow, only their back sticking out above the snow once in a while.

I said to the Supervisor, "Here is a chance to take home a live goat without much trouble." Mr. Haines was skeptical and said I couldn't handle one of the big goats alone. If I picked a real small one, we might get one to the station between us. I told him, "Just watch my smoke." I was in good shape in them days and didn't take my hat off for nobody.

Anyhow, I cut across with my snowshoes and headed the goats off before they reached the shore and fell on the nearest goat that was handy. It happened to be a good-sized one at that. There were goats everywhere in that narrow trench, one climbing over another to get away and no time for a selection.

I thought I surprised the goats, but the surprise was on me. I was on top of the goat when I started trying to hang onto his head. The next thing I knew I was on the bottom and the goat on top. I had snow and goat hair and whatnot in my eyes and down my neck. He tried his darndest to hook me with his sharp horns, and I had my hands full to keep him from hooking me in the face or other parts of the body. His feet got lodged in the webbing of my snowshoes and tore most of the webbing out. Half of my pants and coat was already gone when the Supervisor came up to help me. But what did he do? Lay down in the snow and laughed until the tears ran down his cheeks, and me getting more mad every minute. Finally one snowshoe came off, and not long afterwards the other. After that I could handle him better and straddled his back and just watched out for his horns. He could kick like a mule, but his hoofs were not as sharp as those of a deer. I rode the blooming goat back and forth in that ditch until he was plumb petered out, and the Supervisor yelling, "Ride him cowboy!"

I told the Supervisor to bring my pack sack and what was left of my pants. I had some rope in the pack sack and fixed up one of my broken snowshoes and tied a piece of rope around the goat's horns and one piece around his hind leg. I thought we could lead him home. It worked fine in the deep snow and on the ice and while the goat was still petered out. But when we hit the timber and solid footing, the goat changed tactics. He was leading us instead of us leading him. The Supervisor was hanging onto the rope to keep the billy from running over me. Once or twice he couldn't hang onto his rope and the goat charged me, and I had the choice either to play hide and seek behind a tree or lose another piece of my pants, which by the way, the Supervisor said "belonged to the Adam and Eve variety." I tried to put my coat over his head. I thought he would lead better but in the shuffle the rope came off his hind legs. After that he was too dangerous to handle. In a split second he had got himself tangled up in the brush with the rope on his horns. After a struggle I managed to cut the rope and set him free. It was just as well. If we had to tug the goat another mile we would have had no clothes left on us except our rubbers and socks, and they were all wringing wet.

The very next spring I packed a goat kid from above the station in my pack sack. But as he refused to drink any milk, in a couple of days I packed him back up again on the hillside where several nanny goats and kids were feeding. I had quite a time getting rid of the kid, as he tried to follow me. I finally stuck him behind some big rocks and ran a little distance, and when the little fellow couldn't find me he wandered off. When the big nanny goats spotted the little kid running around, they came over to investigate. When they got near enough that the little kid could see them he ran over to one of the big nannies and wanted his dinner right away. But she bumped him so hard that he rolled over several times. Another nanny came up and smelled him all over, bumped him once or twice but not very hard, and by good luck took him over and let him have some of her milk. Boy, was the little fellow hungry! It was a sight worth seeing and I swore never to take a little goat home again. I had dozens of chances afterwards. I even had young mountain sheep in my hands but I never took one away.

Frank Liebig told his mountain goat story to *Outdoor Life*. OUTDOOR LIFE.

Ed Stahl, Fred Herrig, and Bruno. HERRIG FAMILY COLLECTION.

FIVE

A SPELL OVER THE LAND

Along about 1903 or so, a spell fell over the land. No one was sure just how or when it happened, and opinion was split on whether the spell was cast by angels or demons. The adventuresome rangers, lumbermen, miners, and settlers, who had been content to go it alone for many years and had satisfied the stirring in their loins in the houses and cribs of Montana's brothels, were having strange new desires. They wanted wives and families. First one and then another fell under the spell.

Many of these men were immigrants who had left all of their kinsmen in Europe. There was no family here to pull around them, like a warm blanket, as they grew old. Maybe they saw into the future and the lonesome nights ahead made them shiver. Or maybe it was simply that their lust for rugged adventures had been satisfied and the time had come to enjoy the soothing embrace of a steady, good woman and the comforts of a warm, kept home. Or, just as their fathers before them, it was time to breed a hardy new line in their ancestral name that would make them immortal.

When Fred Herrig arrived at his new assignment in Fortine in 1903, he staked out the area that was to become the Forestry Station. He had great plans for his new station. He picked out a place for the cabin and decided where he would put up the barns and corrals and what sections of the range land would be suitable to fence and cross-fence for pasture for the saddle horses and pack mules. He had a notion to plant lilacs around and call the place Lilac Hill Forestry Station. The name had a pleasant ring to it, and carved on a wooden sign with Fred Herrig, Esq., just under the station name, it would look right elegant. Fred announced his plans to Frank Liebig, Bryon Henning, and a few other friends when they stopped by to pay him a visit. They all roared with laughter and told Fred to take another look—the patch of ground he was calling "lilac" was covered with ant hills, and a more fittin' name was Ant Flats. The name stuck. Fred built a cabin and settled into his duties as the ranger of the Ant Flat Forestry Station.

One spring day in 1903, Fred rode out from Ant Flats, dressed in his finest trappings. He had polished his boots, trimmed and waxed his handlebar mustache, curried his bay horse, and combed out Bruno's long wolfhound hair. They made a fine parade as they trotted along the old stage road through the mountains and valleys. It was apparent to anyone he passed that Fred was on a serious mission. He went along the trail to Trego and through the narrow pass at the summit of Stryker, pausing at the signs at the turnouts that read "stop and holler" as warnings to freight wagons to wait to pass. He went on past Radnor and Olney and Whitefish and on to Bad Rock Canyon on the Flathead River between Columbia Falls and Apgar.

Fred had started out early, camped out one night, and then spruced himself up again for his arrival at the homestead of the widow Frieda Wilke. Fred had met Frieda while he was ranger of the Upper North Fork of the Flathead. The *spell* was cast. He got the tingles every time he saw Frieda, and at forty-three he decided it was time to become a husband. Frieda had five small boys who needed a father, and Fred was

ready to take on that job too. After a reasonable courtship he proposed and the wedding day was set.

Fred rode to Columbia Falls for the ceremony with Bruno at his side. The ceremony went fine, but the honeymoon not so well according to a 1972 article by Carol Cannon in the *Montana Magazine of the Northern Rockies*. After the wedding, Fred, the new Mrs. Herrig, and the five boys returned to the Wilke homestead. The Herrig's would honeymoon while gathering up her household goods, cattle, and chickens, and moving the whole lot by wagons and horses to Ant Flats. It would take about three weeks of steady work.

The Wilke family dog and Bruno were introduced to each other during the courtship, but neither one of them appeared interested in a friendship. Now that the Wilkes and Herrigs were joined permanently, there was the matter of territorial rights to be settled. While Fred was enjoying his first supper as a married man and head of a family, the threatening growls of Bruno and the Wilke's dog erupted into a vicious fight under the table. They rolled into a ball of savage, snapping, snarling fur, overturned the table, and were about to do some real damage to the place and to each other when Fred finally yanked them apart.

He took them outside and stationed each one at opposite ends of the yard to cool down and think the situation over. The next morning Bruno was gone. Three weeks later Fred, Frieda, and the five boys reached Ant Flats with wagons loaded with furnishings, caged squawking chickens, and tired cattle.

Fred had left Ed Stahl in charge while he was away. Ed told him that Bruno had returned to the ranger station and had stayed until three days before Fred returned.

Bruno was as flamboyant and adventuresome a creature as Fred Herrig. He had been Fred's constant companion since he was a pup. He had kept watch for the ranger, chased bears and mountain lions away from their night camps, warned Fred of approaching men, and sniffed out the trails of men and animals Fred hunted. He had stood growling sentry while Fred made it plain to timber thieves and game poachers to clear out. He was top dog in the forest, but he smelled change in the air.

Fred had himself a new companion and she had five sons. A hound of Bruno's dignity was not about to be mauled by five little boys and there was that loathsome children's pet to contend with. Maybe Bruno still had the call to roam, or perhaps he too had fallen under the *spell* that drifted over the land and was out scouting up a mate of his own. He disappeared and was never seen again.

By chance there may be some Bruno in the forlorn howl of a wolf on Kintla Peak or in the yipping call of a coyote in the Swiftcurrent Valley.

Fred and Frieda, the five boys, and the Wilke family pet settled in at Ant Flats. That same year, in May, President Roosevelt attended a reception in Butte, Montana. Fred rode over to Butte and joined the group of Rough Riders that had shown up for the occasion. Ten thousand people gathered to greet the president as he stood on the balcony of the Finlen Hotel to give a speech. Roosevelt scanned the ranks of the Rough Riders in the audience and called out, "Is Fred Herrig here? I want Fred Herrig. Oh, there you are. Come up here, Fred. I want you here." When Fred got to the balcony, Roosevelt gave him a hearty handshake and said, "This sure beats embalmed beef, doesn't it, Fred!" Fred stood by his side throughout the speech and the presentations. Later, a reporter grabbed Fred and got him to talking about the president. The following interview was reported in the *Anaconda Standard* of May 31, 1903.

> *Roosevelt was never afraid of work himself. In fact, he wouldn't let any of us do anything for him. He would put out his own horse and saddle his own horse, and if he chanced to be first to camp or if the others were busy, he would make the fire and start the cooking. He was a good camp cook. He wanted nobody to wait on him. He was just as independent then as he is now. He was always jolly in camp and was mighty good company.*
>
> *When Roosevelt first came to the Little Missouri, there was a disposition among some to make a little fun of him. There was a prejudice against any tenderfoot just arrived from the East, especially against a man with glasses. But Roosevelt made himself popular right away and was greatly liked by all the cowboys and people there.*

I remember the first election we had there and what Roosevelt said to me. It was when the county was first organized. I had been working on a ranch eight miles below Roosevelt's.

There were just fifteen votes all told. Howard Eaton of the ranch where I was working, and Savin Ferris of the Roosevelt ranch were running for county commissioner. I had promised Eaton that I would vote for him. Before the election I was hired to work on the Roosevelt ranch. Ferris asked me to vote for him but I told him I had promised Eaton my vote. It was known that the vote would be seven for each candidate, with my vote to decide which should be elected. Ferris went to Roosevelt about it and Roosevelt came to me and asked how I was going to vote. I told him I was going to vote for Eaton, as I had promised, and he said, "I would like to have you vote for us, but if you promised Eaton, that is the man you should vote for. Stick to your word."

The day before election our bunch of saddle horses got away and our foreman thought they would strike for the Powder River country where they were raised. That was three hundred miles away. So he asked Roosevelt to send me after them, so I could not be on hand to vote. But Roosevelt said, "No. We can wait 'til election is over. Fred has a right to put in his vote." Eaton won the election but Roosevelt won the county.

Fred was almighty proud of his friendship with Roosevelt. It was high praise to be a close friend of such an honorable man. Nothing else that Fred would do would mean as much to him. When Roosevelt died in 1919, it was plain to everyone that Fred had a suffering heart. The nation had lost a fine man and he a good friend.

Fred was a member of the Roosevelt Rough Riders Association, and not even the fires of 1910 kept him from attending the reunion. He was also involved with the Roosevelt Memorial Association and in getting pensions established for the veterans of the Spanish-American War.

The Forest Service was still pressuring Fred to become one of the "new breed of Forest Ranger." Instead of working mostly as a law officer, they insisted he learn something about forestry. It was with great reluctance that Fred rode over to see Frank Liebig sometime in 1905 to get lessons on surveying and scaling timber. Since Fred had been the teacher about the lawman part of the ranger's job back in 1902, Frank was pleased to teach him about the forestry part of the job.

Fred considered it dull duty, but he learned how to survey and scale timber and as much about trees, shrubs, and forest insects as Frank could cram into him. Then he returned to his district and made a show of his new skills to his supervisor. Fred never considered himself one of the new breed, but he did manage to keep the Forest Service satisfied and himself on the payroll for the next twenty-two years.

During World War I, Fred was deputized to guard the troop trains that went through Montana. It was extra duty for rangers but more to his liking than scaling timber. It gave him occasion to bend the ears of the eager young soldiers about the Spanish-American War and Roosevelt.

Fred's son, Robert, was born in 1907. Robert married the Lincoln County librarian, Inez Ratekin. Robert and Fred's stepson Bert Wilke followed in Fred's footsteps and had distinguished careers in the Forest Service.

Fred continued to serve as the ranger at the Ant Flat Station until 1927 when he retired. He had the distinction of being the first ranger in the Flathead and Kootenai Forests and having served longer at one station than anyone in the Forest Service.

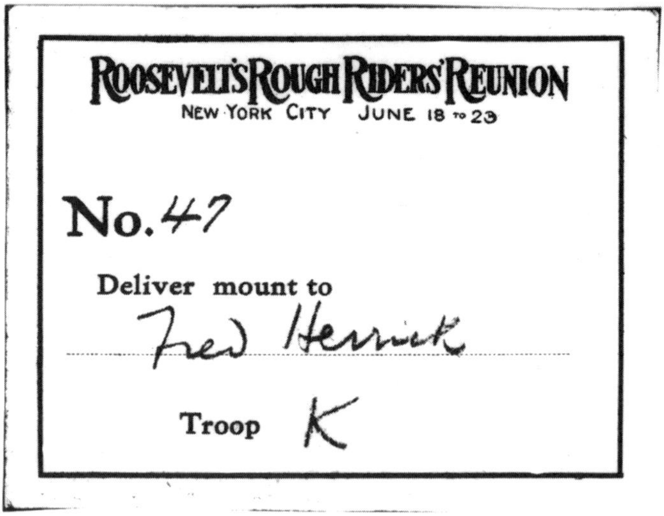

Rough Riders Reunion card. HERRIG FAMILY COLLECTION.

SIX

LULU— A RANGER'S WIFE AND LIFE

Wedding bells were ringing all over the northwest wilderness. The cabins of long-time bachelors had curtains in the windows and children playing in the yards. They could offer a visitor a slice of savory roast with herb gravy and potatoes, coffee or tea, and wild berry pie for dessert when they dropped by, instead of a bowl of survival stew, whiskey, and a hard biscuit. Yes, change was in the air, and for Frank Liebig too.

In 1888, George R. McMahon, an upholsterer in Waukesha, Wisconsin, his wife Jessie Fremont and their infant daughter Lulu May came west. They had been lured by tales of the beauty and the promise of opportunity in the northwest from Jessie's brother Freeman Wedge who had homesteaded in Columbia Falls, Montana, in 1884. The McMahons got as far as Helena when the brutal winter of 1888–1889 closed in around them. George took a job as a mortician and the McMahons waited out the bitterly cold, snowbound months in Helena. At the first sign of spring in 1889, George quit his job, and he and Jessie loaded their goods and their wriggling one-year old daughter Lulu into a covered wagon. They waved tearful goodbyes to the hard winter's accumulation of friends and continued their trek north. The wagon lurched, rolled, and clattered along the narrow mud-rutted trails through the mountains and into the Flathead Valley, finally stopping at the homestead of Jessie's brother Freeman near Columbia Falls.

The McMahons and Wedges at the Wedge homestead in Columbia Falls.
LIEBIG COLLECTION.

Jessie had been born the fifteenth of sixteen children in the Wedge family. She, just as her mother before her, had plans for a large family gathered about her. Each new child she brought to this earth would add to her fulfillment. She planned to grow old enjoying her children as they grew and blossomed and their lives unfolded before her like those of the heroes and heroines in the great novels she had read. Soon after they arrived in Columbia Falls, she gave birth to a second daughter, Mamie. Her plans for a large cast of McMahons were well in progress.

George, like his brother-in-law Freeman, had taken up a homestead, built a house, and farmed the land. But weather in the northwest made farming an uncertain venture, and the enterprising George sought

The Wedge homestead in Columbia Falls. LIEBIG COLLECTION.

surer ways to earn money for his growing family. In this wild country, however short on numbers of people and new births, it was relatively long on untimely deaths. Death by gunshot, hanging, drowning, freezing, and lightning were recorded as natural causes. In the 1880s, a mortician in Montana was reasonably certain of steady clientele from one cause or another. George had learned the mortician trade in his winter in Helena. He took up the trade again and founded the Woodlawn Cemetery of Columbia Falls.

In 1891, Columbia Falls began to boom amidst widespread speculation that it was the ideal place for the Great Northern Railway to establish its division point and build its roundhouse to maintain engines needed to pull trains "over the hump" toward the Pacific. Eighteen saloons and numerous retail stores materialized. The first bank was established, several hotels went up, and the *Columbian Newspaper* was published. Land prices jumped. Columbia Falls became a rip-roaring river town.

The mortuary business was profitable for George in one way or another. He was paid for his services, sometimes in money and sometimes with the possessions of the dearly departed if there were no survivors or the survivors were broke, which was frequently the case.

Anything from chairs to books, shovels to wagons, and Mackinaws to saddlebags were offered to cover funeral expenses. It wasn't long until George had a little money and a mountain of stuff he didn't need. The ever-resourceful George opened a secondhand store and sold the dearly departeds' goods.

Later he joined the volunteer fire department and took an interest in the political affairs of the city. The McMahons were becoming a prominent Columbia Falls family. In the meantime, Jessie's plan for a large family was moving right along. She brought the third McMahon daughter into the world, and George named her Jessie after her mother.

Jessie and George often took their Sunday outings in a horse-drawn sleigh or wagon and visited Jessie's brother and his family on their farm. But often as not, after Sunday church services, they strolled through the exciting, fast-growing and wild town of Columbia Falls. George carried Mamie and tipped his hat at passersby, and Jessie carried the infant Jess and nodded "Good afternoon." The bright-eyed Lulu toddled along beside them hanging to her mother's skirts or holding her father's hand.

As Lulu grew older, she would remember the scenes of those early days in Columbia Falls and especially the watering trough where the old freighters stopped to water their horses when the Great Northern Railroad was being built across one corner of the place. *I can remember the excitement and activity of seeing all this and the horse-drawn scrapers and men with picks and shovels as I watched from a distance.* She also recalled *that old school building, the Columbus, is where I attended first grade and used to walk all that distance from our home.*

Columbia Falls's bid for prosperity plummeted when the Great Northern Railway decided to build the main route through Kalispell and make Whitefish its base of operations. In 1894, George, with his accustomed resourcefulness, packed up and moved to Kalispell. There, as in Columbia Falls, he established a mortuary and a secondhand store and soon joined the fire department. He was also able to acquire a bit of property that he rented out.

Jessie had their fourth daughter, Kathryn. The four engaging little girls were her great joy, and she was working on producing some boys to help George in the business and carry on the McMahon name. But

Jessie did not have the vigorous health and good luck of her mother in bearing children. In 1896, she died in terrible pain from the rupturing birth of their stillborn son. Lulu was eight when Jessie died and old enough to remember her mother's agony on that sad day and her father's torment during the months to come.

Lulu in her youth, 1906. LIEBIG COLLECTION.

A hard, mournful year later, the busy widower, with four small girls to raise, found love again with the daughter of a local farm family and married Elizabeth Gilmour. Lulu grew up helping her stepmother care for her sisters and finishing school in Kalispell.

The winter of 1906 and 1907 in the Rockies was brutal. January was paralyzingly cold and winds blew thirty to forty miles per hour. Blizzard snows covered freight and passenger trains from Cut Bank on the east side of the Rockies to Essex on the western slope. The trains' wheels froze to their journal bearings. It took almost a week to break through the snow and clear the tracks so that the trains could get through. The snow in Frank Liebig's ranger district was too deep to do any work. He left his cabin at the head of Lake McDonald and went to Kalispell to work out of ranger headquarters for a month or two. He rented a small house from Mr. McMahon. Frank spent his off-duty time in Kalispell fixing his gear for the coming spring, reading, studying the plants he collected, visiting with the town folks, and taking advantage of the passing travelers to catch up on the news in the rest of the country.

George McMahon took a liking to the quiet ranger and invited Frank over for dinner. Two of George's four daughters were of marriageable age. A forthright, single gentleman with steady work was most certainly welcome at the McMahon's table.

At nineteen, Lulu had grown into a fine-figured woman with handsome features. She had a thin straight nose and smooth oval face. The gentle warmth of her deep soulful eyes overpowered the unaccountable wistfulness that posed on her thin smile. It was as if she had endured some tragic sadness in a past life that had forged in her a great empathy in this one. But Lulu's soulful eyes and quiet elegance also masked an active imagination and a spirit that yearned for more adventure than what ordinarily came to the simple lives of the good women of Kalispell. Lulu imagined herself challenging nature as Fay Fuller had done when she climbed Mount Rainier and was heralded as the first woman to top the snow-covered peak. At times, when the stories about Elizabeth Collins were being talked about all over Kalispell, she thought she too might like to create a ranching empire like the forceful Cattle Queen of Montana. Her most lavish dreams were when she pictured herself as another Julia Marlowe bowing to standing applause for her banner performances on the stage. Lulu's dreams of adventure were heightened by a will and resourcefulness that matched her father's. She was sure that she could meet any challenge and survive any hardship and she yearned to try. But battling her dreams for herself was her own paralyzing shyness and her mother's blood flowing through her veins that carried a selfless and consuming love of family.

In the early West, men far outnumbered the women, and in the early 1900s it was still the case, although somewhat more in balance. "Wife Wanted" signs were still posted on cabin doors. Kalispell was a typical western town of the 1900s. It was the center of a large male population of railroad men, ranchers, rangers, bankers, and shopkeepers. A fair, young woman who could cook and sew was highly prized and courted to a fare-thee-well. Lulu May McMahon had turned away many a hopeful suitor holding on to the dreams of her own secret world.

George McMahon, with a conspiratorial smile, introduced his four daughters to Ranger Liebig, who was renting the McMahon's little house for the winter months. Lulu thought the ranger rather handsome and he had an intriguing foreign accent. George seated Frank at the table and Elizabeth, who usually had Lulu serve the dinner, announced that she would serve and George and the girls should take their places at the table. Frank sat across the table from Lulu and appeared to be enjoying the slices of rare beef and the garden beans and boiled potatoes that were brought up from the McMahon's canning and root cellar for the occasion. During dinner, George and Elizabeth's lightly veiled questioning of the German immigrant served as conversation.

Frank was amused. It was obvious he was here to meet the eligible McMahon daughters. That was quite all right with him—he had seen the girls in town and was somewhat taken with Lulu May. The *spell* that had turned Fred Herrig and some of the other rangers into romantics a few years earlier seemed to have settled on him too. The usually taciturn Frank Liebig talked freely about himself.

During dinner, with the help of Elizabeth's spurring the ranger to talk about himself, Lulu decided he was the most interesting of the gentlemen her father had invited for dinner in the last couple of years. He was not tall, but he seemed so. He was certainly strong, both in character and physique. His taut, sinewy muscles showed through the wool shirt and in the effortless way he moved. His commanding will showed in the lift of his head and in his cool, penetrating eyes. He had the courage to venture from his homeland, an ocean away. He had the good sense to know he needed American schooling to get by in his adopted country. He apparently could do anything he set his mind to. He had been a cowboy and ranch foreman, a logger, a surveyor, and a man who lived off the land. He was thirty-five and a ranger for the U.S. Forest Service, which was a highly respected position. Throughout dinner, Lulu became more and more fascinated by the man seated across from her. She helped Elizabeth clear the dinner dishes and serve dessert. She surprised herself when she passed Frank a piece of pie and gave him a pleasing smile and the full power of her warming eyes.

The invitation for dinner was repeated several times and Frank gladly accepted. Some evenings Frank invited himself over for a game of cards or to sit and talk around the fire. Frank and Lulu went for sleigh rides, strolled the streets of Kalispell, and sat on the porch and talked. They exchanged warming glances over dinner at the McMahons and sat shoulder-to-shoulder at Sunday services at the First Presbyterian Church on Second Avenue.

Winter's gray mantle still covered the northwest and the snow was still deep when Frank had to return to his ranger district in the Glacier country and begin his patrols. For the next few months, Lulu wrote to Frank, and Frank used every opportunity to make a trip into Kalispell to see her. He delivered his monthly ranger's report in person rather than mail it to headquarters in Kalispell. Supervisor Haines saw more of Frank that year than he ever had before or since.

Frank and Lulu were married June 6, 1907. They honeymooned at the Belton Hotel and then went to the ranger station on Lake McDonald to begin their life together.

Unlike many women starting life in the wilderness, Lulu did not have to start out in a tent, a sod house, or a floor-less cabin. The Mount Stanton Ranger Station was a snug two-room log cabin. It was, however, the habitat of a long-time, often out-on-the-trail, bachelor. The mounted heads of goats and deer and the antlers of elk, moose, and antelope decorated the walls, along with maps of the area that Frank used in his work. The hides of mountain sheep and bear covered the floors and made soft throws over hard wooden chairs. The furnishings included a cast iron cookstove that also provided the heat, a steamer trunk, a sawbuck table, and various chairs and a wood-framed bed. One corner of the cabin was boxed in to make a darkroom for developing the pictures of wildlife that Frank photographed on the trail.

Lulu was content. She liked having her own home. It was primitive compared to her father's house in Kalispell, but it was hers and Frank's and she would make it comfortable. She scrubbed the wooden walls and floors and tables and chairs until they were shades lighter, and the

Belton, Montana, 1907. GLACIER NATIONAL PARK ARCHIVES.

Inside the Mount Stanton Ranger Station.
PHOTOGRAPH BY FRANK LIEBIG. LIEBIG COLLECTION.

Inside the Mount Stanton Ranger Station.
PHOTOGRAPH BY FRANK LIEBIG. LIEBIG COLLECTION.

Lulu on the porch of the Mount Stanton Ranger Station.
PHOTOGRAPH BY FRANK LIEBIG. LIEBIG COLLECTION.

scent of cedar after a rainfall lingered in the air. She made curtains for the windows and drapes to hang in the doorway between the bedroom and her kitchen. She set out the embroidered tablecloths and dishtowels and made up the bed with crochet-trimmed pillowcases and neatly quilted comforters from her hope chest. She left Frank's mounted specimens where he had placed them, and she added a few knick-knacks and family pictures of her own.

Lulu had learned to cook as a child. When her mother died, she helped her father as much as an eight-year-old was capable. George had hired a housekeeper, but Lulu often cooked for him in the evenings and helped the housekeeper with the cleaning and tending her baby sisters. She was already a good cook when she married Frank, and she quickly expanded her artistry from beef, fish, and chicken to venison, elk, goat, and bear. She helped Frank butcher, smoke, and cure wild game and became a good hand at it herself. She gathered herbs in the forest to season the game and root plants to add to savory bear stews. When her mouth watered for fresh fish she took a pole, went to the lake, and caught trout for their dinner.

Frank and Lulu's supply of meat was always on hand in the forest, but clothing and necessary staples were carried in on backpacks or horseback. The freight from Kalispell to Belton was twenty-five cents per hundred pounds and another twenty-five cents per hundred from Belton to the head of Lake McDonald. In those days, twenty-five cents could buy much-needed canning jars or wool cloth, so they packed their groceries in themselves and bought the extra jars and cloth. In winter, they put on backpacks and snowshoes and came around the lake along the shore, or if the lake was frozen they walked across it. In summer, they used the pack animals and brought in bigger loads.

Lulu often went with Frank out on the trails. She had noticed the numerous tracks of marten on the high trails and set a trap line, which she ran herself. Martens were a good price, and her luck ran well enough that furnishings and other extras were bought for the cabin. They purchased pipe and pumped water in from the lake, putting an end to carrying it in buckets, and she coaxed Frank into adding a room to the cabin. She planted a few bright wildflowers in pails to set on the porch.

The continuous threat of grizzlies and mountain lions in the area did not deter her from fishing the streams, picking wild berries, or walking a good many miles with fresh-baked berry cobbler to

Frank, Lulu, Miss Plank, and her niece
at the Mount Stanton Ranger Station, 1907. LIEBIG COLLECTION.

pay a visit to an ailing neighbor. Lulu bested the hardships of their primitive living, and she was rather proud of her accomplishments. Cattle queens, actresses, or conquerors of mountains could not have done better.

One time late in the fall, Lulu and Frank were camped on Mineral Creek doing trail work when the first snowstorm of the season came on them. It dropped out of the sky like the housekeepers of Heaven had suddenly shook the stuffing out of a thousand giant feather beds. The feathery flakes glided silently to earth, forming layers of white blankets piled one on top of the other, growing higher and higher. Frank and Lulu huddled together in their small tent, watching the snow fall, sipping water and cold coffee from jugs, eating a dinner of jerked bear meat and bread, and talking about one thing and another. Night came with no letup in the falling snow. They lit candles and read from a book they had brought along, then crawled into the warmth of their bedrolls. Lulu had grown accustomed to life on the trail. She was a hearty worker and a big help to Frank on trail work and setting up camp. This time she was also four months pregnant, and Frank was cautious about what he let her do. He made her stay snug in her blankets while he got up several times during the night, put his coat on, and shoveled away the snow that threatened to crush the tent. By daylight he had carved a cave around the tent and woke Lulu. They took down the tent and packed up their goods.

It was early in the season, and Frank had not brought along snowshoes for Lulu. There was no way she could walk through the snow without falling in over her head. Frank started digging a channel through the eleven feet of snow that had fallen. As the morning wore on Frank worked himself into a good sweat throwing snow right and left. Frank dug as fast as he could, but progress through the heavy snow was still slow. It was well toward noon by the time he had cut a channel through the deepest places and finally reached ground where the snow had settled and was only waist high. They trudged another ten miles to a snowshoe cabin, with Frank shoveling away the snow in his path and inventing choice words for Montana weather. Lulu followed along in his path, anxious to get to the warmth and safety of the cabin but

Frank's tent pitched in what he recorded as eleven feet of snow, near Mineral Creek, 1908. PHOTOGRAPH BY FRANK LIEBIG. LIEBIG COLLECTION.

occasionally breaking into an unmuffled giggle at Frank's mumbling about tricky weather that tried to outsmart him. They spent the night enjoying the comfort of the cabin, then headed back to Lake McDonald.

Lulu spent many nights alone in the cabin at Lake McDonald. Frank was out on the trails and often could not make it home by dark. The windfall from a storm would trap him and it would take hours to clear the trail again to get out. He always carried a tent on the back of his horse, and on those occasions he camped out. Lulu knew what it was like on the trail and was not one to fret over Frank's absence. She knew Frank could take care of himself.

One night, Frank's saddle horse, Injun, came in alone with the reins dragging, and that set her to worrying. Something must have happened to Frank for Injun to be on the loose. It was deadly dark and there was no one around. She knew she couldn't backtrack in the blackness of the night. She unsaddled Injun and put him in the corral and gave him some feed. Then she hung a lantern on the porch and made herself a pot of coffee. She sat at the table sipping her coffee and reminding herself how unlikely it was that anything serious would happen to Frank in the mountains he knew so well. When morning broke through the darkness, she dressed in riding clothes and packed some camping and medical supplies. She could ride over to Kelly's or Geduhn's and ask them to look for Frank, or she could try to backtrack herself. Frank would be mightily embarrassed if he was not hurt and somehow had only lost his horse and Kelly and Geduhn came galloping up to his rescue. It would be a good laugh on Ranger Liebig and the talk of Lake McDonald. Lulu decided she better try backtracking herself. She was saddling the horse when the form of the chagrined Ranger Liebig came walking through the trees. He nodded a greeting to a relieved and smiling Lulu, took the reins from her, said a few harsh words in German to Injun and led the horse back to the corral. The incident was never mentioned by Frank, and Injun never came back without him again. For months afterward, a thin smile crossed Lulu's face when she thought about it, but she never told the story of *Ranger Liebig accidentally afoot* until many years later.

By March 1908, Frank and Lulu's first child was about ready to make an appearance. Lulu packed a duffel with the infant blankets, clothes, and diapers she had made and some clothes for herself and Frank. She could have stayed in the cabin at the lake and asked one of the women settlers to help with the delivery of her baby and counted herself as among the bona fide pioneer women who had no choice and left much to chance, but Lulu remembered too well the tragic fate of her mother and baby brother. She intended to have her child in the presence of the family doctor in Kalispell. It would take at least two days to get from the cabin on Lake McDonald to the doctor in Kalispell *if* she made the train connections out of Belton. She judged her time, and Frank took her to her father's home in Kalispell three days ahead of when she expected the baby to be born. It was another three days of waiting and nervous anticipation before their first daughter, Jean, was born on March 16. When Jean was three weeks old, Lulu bundled her up, and Frank and Lulu showed her off to old friends in Kalispell, the Wedge family in Columbia Falls, and the long-time settlers in Belton, then took her back to the cabin at the head of Lake McDonald.

In the winter that followed, Jean was just big enough to toddle around the cabin. One cold day, Frank was outside working and Jean was playing quietly in a corner of the cabin. Lulu added salt to the pot of venison stew simmering on the stove and rolled out dough for biscuits and set them into a pan. She stoked the fire in the stove and stepped outside to bring in more wood. She had an armload of wood gathered when she heard Jean screaming inside the cabin. She dropped the wood and ran inside.

The door to the firebox of the stove was open, a burning splinter of wood was on the floor and Jean's wool dress ablaze. Flames were rushing toward her face. Lulu grabbed up a hide from one of the chairs and wrapped it around Jean to smother the fire. Frank had heard the screams and bolted through the door just as Lulu patted out the last flames from the burning dress. Frank tossed the burning splinter into the stove and shut the box, then knelt to hold the flaying arms of his terrified daughter while Lulu gently tore the smoldering clothing away from her burned body. Jean wailed in agony. She had severe burns under her arm and along her side. Lulu's medicine box was stocked with the usual remedies for life in the wilderness—sulphur, castor oil, powdered alum, whiskey, herbs for poultices, and an assortment of ointments—but she had no medicine to treat such a serious burn or ease Jean's terrible pain. They risked a few sips of whiskey to dull some of the pain, but it gave little relief. They had to get her to a doctor immediately. The snow was three feet deep. The fastest way to get Jean to a doctor was to carry her across the frozen Lake McDonald to Belton. Lulu tore up a cotton sheet and carefully wrapped it around Jean, then Frank eased the swaddled, crying child into his backpack. He put on his snowshoes, and Lulu helped him carefully hoist Jean onto his back. He headed out across the lake, breaking a trail through the snow. Lulu stuffed some clothes for the baby and themselves into a pack, closed up the cabin, then followed in Frank's tracks. The cries of their suffering child pressed them on at lung-bursting speed through the thirteen miles of snow-covered frozen lake to Belton. Fortunately, there was a doctor in Belton by then. He immediately gave the baby girl an anesthetic. While she slept, he cut away the burned flesh and applied antiseptics and salves to the exposed wounds. It took a long time and Lulu's careful nursing to heal the burns. Jean was too young at the time to later remember the pain, but the scars remained.

The Liebig girls in a packing crate.
PHOTOGRAPH BY FRANK AND LULU LIEBIG. LIEBIG COLLECTION.

By 1909, Frank's ranger station began to fill with little women. Their second daughter, Frances, was born in October in Kalispell and, just as with her sister Jean, brought to the cabin on Lake McDonald when she was about three weeks old. The lively toddler and the infant girl kept Lulu in a whirlwind of motherly work and brought a new sound to the wild lands; the velvet laughter of little girls.

New Sounds in the Wild Lands

One winter night, Jean was walking around the cabin, looking out through the windows, watching for her dad to come home from trail work. The full moon cast a silvery glow on the deep crystalline snow around the cabin. It was nearly as bright as day except for the shadowy cedars standing dark and scary in the background. Jean waited at one window and then another, watching anxiously for the form of her father to come through the trees. Lulu sat in a chair by the stove, stitching a tear in Frank's shirt. Frannie was asleep in the wooden box that served as her cradle. Suddenly Jean let out a terrified scream. Lulu's head snapped up. She looked toward the window. The menacing face and deadly stalking eyes of a large mountain lion looked in. Lulu grabbed up Jean

Left: One of the Liebig daughters. PHOTOGRAPH BY FRANK AND LULU LIEBIG. LIEBIG COLLECTION.

Right: Frank packing his daughters Jean and Frances. PHOTOGRAPH BY LULU LIEBIG. LIEBIG COLLECTION.

and set her in the corner away from the window next to where Frannie lay sleeping. Lions rarely came close to the cabins unless game was seriously scarce, and that year it was. The lion may have been attracted by the movements of the small girls and considered them an easy meal. Lulu didn't know, but she was certain the big lion could crash through the window if he took the notion. They were not safe, even in the cabin. She got Frank's rifle from the rack on the wall. Her hands trembled as she fumbled with the shells trying to jam them into the chamber. She watched the windows as she loaded and yelled at Jean to stay put. When she got the rifle loaded, she stood stock still in the middle of the room with the rifle aimed at the window. The lion appeared again, then as quickly disappeared. She feared that his next move would be to leap through the glass into the room. Lulu held her breath, waiting for the massive head and body of the cat to come crashing in.

She exhaled then slowly breathed in and out as a drumbeat of long terrifying minutes passed by. Her arms grew weary from the weight of the aimed rifle. The barrel began to drop and she had to muster the strength to raise it again. Jean whimpered in the corner.

What seemed a long time went by, and the lion did not appear in the window. Lulu began to feel confident he was not going to make a run at the cabin. She went cautiously to the window and looked out. The lion was not there. She hurriedly looked through all the windows and it was nowhere in sight. Lulu took a deep breath. She leaned the rifle against the cabin wall and picked up Jean to comfort her, then she paced the cabin, looking through each window as she passed. Frank would be home any minute.

When Frank rode in, Lulu set Jean down and rushed to the doorway to call out a warning in case the lion was still stalking the cabin. Frank nodded his understanding, drew his rifle out of the scabbard as he dismounted and looked around for the lion. In the bright moonlight, it was easy to see the large tracks leading to the cabin, circling it, then heading back through the woods toward Stanton Mountain. Frank unsaddled Injun and turned him loose in the corral, then returned to the cabin and Lulu's relieved, welcoming embrace.

The lion had become a threat to Lulu and the children. The next morning Frank began the hunt. He also decided that he had better bring in some more deer meat for the winter. He was getting low on venison; the deer were getting scarce and the season was fast running out. In those days, deer season ended on the first of January.

Frank tracked the lion through the forest and along the ridges at the base of the mountain. He found several deer kills where the lion had made a meal and left the rest for the coyotes. As he scouted the area, he counted up the kills that the lion had made in what he guessed was about a three-week period by the state of the carcasses. The lion had killed twenty deer and scared off most of the rest. On the grassy slopes where Frank often saw large numbers of deer, there were none in sight.

The lion tracks led straight up the mountain and Frank followed. About halfway up, he found hot sign leading to a cliff that stood perpendicular to him and about twenty feet above his head.

He had the advantage of the wind and climbed slowly, carefully, and quietly up the ridge. As he approached a clump of growth under the cliff, he caught a glimpse of movement. He crept closer. The lion was lying on the edge of a large boulder, its long tail swinging silently back and forth, ready to pounce on anything that came along on the trail beneath. The lion suddenly jumped, twisting in the air to turn toward him. Frank's first shot brought the lion off the cliff with a scream. As the lion crashed through the brush below he gave it another shot to be sure.

Frank skinned the big male cat out and carried the skin home. It is mounted and part of the wildlife collection in Glacier National Park.

A Ranger Family's Christmas

One cold December day, Frank went to Belton for the mail. The lake was frozen over and the snow had blown off the ice. Frank skated the ten miles across the lake, then put on his snowshoes to travel the remaining three miles to Belton. He picked up the mail and ran a few errands. The next day was Christmas and he wanted to bring his family some cheer. He went to the mercantile and purchased a crate of oranges for the girls and a hotcake griddle for Lulu. He spent the night in Belton and got up well before daylight. He intended to be home when the children woke up on Christmas day. He strapped the crate of oranges and the griddle to his back and set out on snowshoes. When he reached the lake, he put the hotcake griddle on the ice, set the crate of oranges on top, and tied a short rope to the handle of the griddle. He put on his ice skates and off he went pulling the griddle and oranges across the frozen lake like a sled.

He arrived home in time to set the delightful presents from Santa Claus under the tree before Lulu and the girls woke up. Jean enjoyed eating the sweet, juicy oranges and smearing pulp all over her face. Frannie's oranges were squeezed into juice for her to sip from a cup. Frank and Lulu invited their neighbors over for breakfast and put the griddle to work cooking sourdough hotcakes for their Christmas breakfast. Lulu and Frank became famous around Lake McDonald for making hotcakes on the Christmas griddle, and Ranger Liebig became known as Old Sourdough, a title he did not relish and took some pains to discourage.

Frank and Lulu with daughters (left to right) Margaret, Jean, and Frances, in 1912 or 1913. LIEBIG COLLECTION.

The Ranger's Wife

When forest fires raged in Frank's district or when he was lending a hand to fight fires in other districts, Lulu was often the fire-camp cook. Generally, she cooked the food at her cabin or the closest ranger station. Mules and horses were used to pack the meals into the fire fighters on the line. She had a reputation for getting each meal to them on time. When the fires were too far away to cook in cabins and pack the food in, she got someone to care for her children and set up a cooking station at the fire-camp. She often did double duty as the camp nurse, washing and applying ointments to cuts and burns and wrapping the field-splinted broken bones of injured fire fighters. When the fires were out and the weary, soot-smeared fire fighters started leaving the scene, she packed up her cooking gear and returned to her home and children and started in again on whatever chore she had left undone when the fire call came.

Lulu posing in a tree at Lake McDonald.
PHOTOGRAPH BY FRANK LIEBIG. LIEBIG COLLECTION.

Frank and Lulu moved from their home in Glacier in 1910 when it became a national park and was turned over to park rangers. For the next several years, Frank's work took him to different districts in the Flathead and Kootenai National Forests and they moved often. Each time, Lulu swept out an old cabin or what served as a ranger station and worked it into a comfortable home for her growing family. She had four more children, Margaret in 1912, Lyman in 1916, Erma in 1921, and Carl in 1924.

Jean and Frances both became Montana schoolteachers. Margaret became a nurse. The two boys followed the men of the Liebig line and became woodsmen, and Erma took up her mother's profession of housewife. Frank and Lulu were quite satisfied with them all.

In 1963, the Kalispell *Inter Lake* newspaper ran a story that conveyed the forthright character of Lulu Liebig. She's right up there with Lincoln of Illinois who walked miles to return pennies to a customer.

In 1913, Lulu and Frank lived at Tally Lake Ranger Station. During the summer, Clara Gilbertson of Kalispell was with a group of friends on a Sunday outing at the lake. She brought her sewing with her. Sometime during the afternoon, she lost her thimble. It was a graduation gift and she valued it highly. It was silver and engraved with her initials, CGG,

Frank and Jean with their catch of fish for dinner. LIEBIG COLLECTION.

and the year of her graduation, 1910. Miss Gilbertson mentioned to Lulu that she had lost her thimble. Time passed. Clara Gilbertson married A. H. Prestbye, Frank was reassigned, and he and Lulu and the children moved to Libby. In 1926, a ranger was cleaning the area around the Tally Lake Ranger Station and found two silver thimbles. One was engraved CGG-1910. He gave them to Lulu. She recalled the young Miss Gilbertson who had lost her thimble but she did not know her married name or how to get in touch with her.

Lulu put the thimbles away and occasionally thought of them. In 1963, she read of the death of A. H. Prestbye and noted that his wife's maiden name had been Clara Gilbertson. Lulu wrote a letter of sympathy to Clara and enclosed the two silver thimbles. It was fifty years in the doing, but Lulu had returned the lost thimble.

Stories about Lulu are rare. She did not keep a diary or journal, as Frank had, and her descendants and friends do not recall Lulu talking about herself. We do know that Lulu provided room and board for many of the Forest Service men during the winter when the rangers came in from summer stations. Carl Wetterstrom and his bride Vi boarded at the Liebig home in Kalispell in 1941 while he waited for his assignment as ranger for the Upper Middle Fork District at Java. They remember

Lulu as always working to make life a little better, a little easier, a little more comfortable for her family and for her friends.

The years passed. Lulu's shoulders slumped and she moved slowly. Her smooth, lovely face transformed into an exquisitely lined scrapbook of a woman's hard life in the early West. Her eyes were still bright, and a thin, knowing smile, as though she kept an amusing secret, dimpled her wrinkled face. Lulu died in 1966 at seventy-eight. She is among the gallant women of the Old West who are unsung and little known. She did not conquer a mountain, build a cattle empire, or travel the world as a great actress. She tamed the wilderness into a comfortable home, and she did it time after time, in Glacier, in the Flathead, in the Blackfeet, in the Pend Oreille, and in the Kootenai Forests. Lulu was mistress of a wild country in a wild time. It had been an adventure!

SEVEN

THE LAST FOREST RANGER

The year 1910 is remembered by northwesterners as the year of the Big Blowup, 125 days of pure hell. It was also the year all of Frank's Forest Reserve district was designated Glacier National Park. Ranger Liebig was fighting fires all over his district, and he was soon to be out of a job.

Forest Reserve to National Park

On May 11, 1910, President Taft signed the bill designating the area eastward from the North Fork of the Flathead River to the Blackfeet Indian Reservation and northward of the Great Northern Railroad to the Canadian border as Glacier National Park. This would be Forest Ranger Frank Liebig's last summer in the mountains he loved. The protection of Glacier was being turned over to *Park Rangers*. This was an expected but an ironic turn in Frank's fate. Along with explorer George B. Grinnell and noted author James W Schultz, Frank had been credited with encouraging the movement to give this spectacular country national park status, which would preserve it in its natural state for all time to come.

Transition of the area from a Forest Reserve under the Department of Agriculture to a National Park under the Department of the Interior

Fire camp, Glacier National Park, 1910. LIEBIG COLLECTION.

was gradual. The first Glacier National Park superintendent, Major William J. Logan, did not arrive until August. Meanwhile, Frank kept steady vigil in his district during the worst fire threat in the history of the northwest. Wildfires in Idaho and Montana charred more than three million acres of forest land. The worst of it was in the Coeur d'Alene and Cabinet Mountains along the Idaho-Montana borders, but that year wildfires erupted all over the northwest from Washington to Minnesota *"faster than a man could walk."*

Wildfires of 1910

In Frank's ranger district, dry lightning set off fires that burned 23,000 acres from Ford Creek below Kintla Lake to the Canadian border and from the Flathead River to the Livingston Mountain Range. Careless campers started fires that burned 8,000 acres around Bowman Lake, up both shores to the foot of the mountains, and spot fires accounted for another 19,000 acres along Camas, Dutch, and Anaconda Creeks. Dozens of smaller fires burned throughout the western slopes. In the southern district of the area, 7,600 acres burned above Nyack and 4,000 acres at Red Eagle. The Ole Creek drainage, Fielding, and the southeastern corner of the park as far as Midvale also burned.

In all, more than 100,000 acres burned in the area that became Glacier National Park that year.

The summer started out bad. Spring was warmer than normal and very little rain fell. The snowpack had melted and flowed away. By the beginning of summer, the ground was parched. By July, some 3,000 fires burned in the northwest. Lightning from numerous raging dry thunderstorms torched many of the fires and reckless campers ignited others.

Typical of what was happening in the northwest in that hot, dry-as-tinder summer is this account from Frank's diary.

> Thursday, July 14: *Went up McDonald Creek to the gorge, posted a number of fire warnings and found a small fire started by someone throwing away a match, thence went across McDonald Creek towards the Glacier hotel, and found a small fire where someone had a fire built right in the trail against a rotten stump and it started to spread, got it finely out too, by carrying water, thence went to Lewis's* (Glacier Hotel) *to see if I couldn't find out who camped there.* Later that day Frank discovered a small fire near his ranger station where a careless smoker had emptied the ashes from his pipe.

On Friday, July 15, Frank rode his horse eight miles up the trail to Sperry Glacier Basin and climbed up Lincoln Peak. From there he was able to look out over large portions of the country. He spotted two fires, a large one near Harrison Lake, south of his district, and a smaller one on Little Saint Mary's Creek. He climbed down Lincoln Peak and headed back to Lake McDonald. He took a launch down the lake to Belton and sent a message to Supervisor Haines in Kalispell to contact the ranger in the Harrison Lake district. He rounded up some help from the settlers in Belton, then before it got dark, he got fresh horses, packed firefighting tools and grub, and headed toward the Little Saint Mary's fire. On the way he stopped off at the cabins of the settlers around Lake McDonald and brought the men and their half-grown sons along to help.

Frank led his firefighting crew through the darkening mountain trails toward the fire. He had fought a fire in this area in 1906 and clearing the trail had taken two days then. It was better now but still grown over. He headed in a straight line up the trail, slashing a path through the tangle of underbrush to the fire site. It took hours of grueling work to get there. By the time the exhausted men got to the fire, the sky was lit up with fiery destruction. The heat was intense and sky-high plumes of crackling flames were engulfing the tall trees. Frank unloaded the firefighting equipment from his pack horses, handed it out, and started the men to carving a trench around the perimeter of the fire to starve it of fuel. The weary men worked feverishly, slashing brush and small trees with axes and using crosscut saws to bring down the thick trunks of the old lords of the forest that stood in the path of the burn. They used their horses and their own brute strength to drag the trees away from the fire's path or to position them for a backfire. It took powerful slams of the mattocks into the hard earth and back-breaking, blister-making shoveling of dirt, rocks, and vegetation to cut the trench. The labor was grueling and there was no let up. Burning death snapped at their heels. They worked through the night.

When the trench was complete and the fire corralled and subsiding, Frank and the weary men took a rest, washed their grimy faces in the stream, boiled some coffee, and sipped it while they told stories of the fire fight and chewed on the strips of bear meat Frank had brought along. When they could muster the energy to move again they packed up and headed back to Lake McDonald.

On the other side of the Whitefish Mountain Range, Fred Herrig, and rangers Ed Hamilton and Joe Eastland were leading crews in brave fights against the fires in the forests around Stryker, Trego, and Fortine.

Fred had gone to the Rough Riders Reunion in New York in late June to see his old friend Theodore Roosevelt. It would be the last time they saw each other. An urgent telegram brought him back to Montana to fight the fires of July.

The fire danger of 1910 and the fires of July forced W. B. Greeley, who was in charge of U.S. Forest Service District One in Missoula, to increase his fire fighting force to nearly 3,000 men.

A few were lumberjacks and veteran fire fighters, but most of the added force had no experience fighting fires. They were *"drifters, picked up on the skid rows of Butte and Spokane."* Despite the inexperience of the firefighters and the difficulty of reaching the fire sites, most of the 3,000 fires of July were contained.

August weather was drier and hotter than July and increasing winds added to the threat. More fires broke out and spread rapidly. President Taft ordered the War Department to furnish troops to assist in fighting fires. Several companies were assigned to Forest Service District One in Missoula to assist in the Idaho-Montana border fires, and other companies were dispatched on demand throughout the northwest, including in Glacier.

From August 10 through 19, a thousand rampaging fires erupted throughout the Flathead, Blackfeet, Kaniksu, Lolo, Cabinet, and Clearwater Forests. The Little Saint Mary's and Harrison Lake fires, which were contained in July, erupted again in August when winds whipped the fires to life again. Over 600 acres of forest were burned before Frank, the other forest rangers, and the volunteers could stop it. All over Idaho and Montana, valiant rangers, firemen, soldiers, and volunteers fought the fires to a smoldering standoff. Most of the fires were out or under control within nine days. They had fought one hellfire after another and were too weary to talk. Tired, hollow eyes stared out from grimy, smoke-covered faces as they finally shouldered axes and shovels to go home.

Then on August 20th nature went berserk. Raging, howling, hurricane-force winds started at the Nez Perce National Forest in Idaho and swept through the forests of northern Idaho and western Montana, whipping the smoldering embers of the hard-fought fires of the weeks before into giant, savage forces so fierce as to be described as *a blazing demon.* Wild flaming fury devoured trees, animals, buildings, and the people in its path as it stormed through the valleys, forests, canyons, and mountains. Nothing could stop it—not the thousands of men who were carrying water, trenching, cutting, sawing, and shoveling. The sky was blood red and dimmed with smoke from horizon to horizon. Ash and smoke reached cities as far away as a thousand miles. The worst destruction was along the Idaho-Montana border where the fires swallowed the towns of Wallace and Mullan in Idaho, and Taft, Haugan, and De Borgia in Montana and took the lives of seventy-eight fire fighters and seven others.

On August 22, the screaming winds began to quiet and ebb, temperatures dropped, snow fell in the higher elevations, and gentle rains fell on the forests along the Idaho-Montana border. On that same day, when the fire crews in the Coeur d'Alene and Cabinet Forests finally had reason to smile, Frank was told about a spot fire that had leaped in from the Whitefish Range across the North Fork and was burning near Dutch and Anaconda Creeks. He saddled his horse and rushed to the fire site.

> *I found myself in possession of a large fire. A dry lightning storm and plenty of wind, and I had a real freak of a fire of a few hundred acres before the day was over.*

Frank rode back to the foot of Lake McDonald as quick as the tired, lathered horse could handle the trail and called for help. Newly arrived Park Superintendent Logan dispatched several companies of soldiers, who had arrived in Glacier from Fort William Henry Harrison near Helena and Fort Wright, Oregon, to assist with fighting the fire.

Fortunately, the Glacier Park was established already and money, seems to me was no object then. First thing I knew I had authority to get all the men I could get hold of. I got all the settlers in the North Fork Valley because I knew they were interested to get the fire out as soon as possible, so their homes wouldn't get burned up. Even at that four or five were burned out. I also received a company of militia soldiers and two companies of regular soldiers and equipment.

The fire raged for twenty days, consuming 19,000 acres of the Camas, Dutch, and Anaconda Creek areas before it was finally brought under control. Frank supervised the fire fighting of the unseasoned troops. These recruits were not accustomed to the hurried back-breaking labor of fire fighting with no letup, or the primitive living conditions. Food was packed in and often had to be served cold, and the standard bed for a fire fighter was a blanket or cheap soogan stretched out on rough ground.

The company of militia was doing fine, but the regular soldiers were a flop. The trouble came about, that the militia soldiers received 30 cents an hour and board and the regulars just received their monthly pay, which I believe was only $25 per month. So, the regulars wouldn't work until they got the same pay as the militia. But they never got an increase.

Later in Frank's diary he reported: *Went back to where the soldiers were working to see what they were doing—didn't like the ditching so I showed them how it ought to be done. . . .* Frank also had a time convincing the soldiers that the fiery demon didn't take the Sabbath off so neither could they. He wrote that the soldiers refused to work on Sunday, noting in his diary that the thirty cents an hour they were receiving did not seem to keep them on their feet. After nine days on the fire line, he wrote, *the soldiers getting disgusted and don't work much anymore.*

The rains came in the last days of August and the first days of September and did what thousands of men could not do, reminding them that nature, not man, was still in control. The fires all over Montana and Idaho cooled, and the exhausted and relieved firefighters began the mop-up. Frank surveyed the damage in the Camas-Anaconda Creek area on September 10 and wrote in his diary: *5 moose, l deer, l bear burned up.*

In the last days of September, nature had finally calmed down after her tantrum and the threat of more fires had dwindled under her rains and snows. The park rangers began their slow takeover of the area, and Frank set out to gather up the Forest Service equipment and tools that he had cached in snowshoe cabins and along the trails. He packed the equipment out to the McDonald Ranger Station, then shipped it to Kalispell. On September 18 he reported: *Was ready to go home, found the horses gone, which must have got stampeded by a bear, as the evidence showed, couldn't find the horses that evening so had to stay there overnight.*

When the gear was all collected, Frank joined some other rangers and rode up the North Fork to the Canadian border, inspecting and surveying boundaries on homestead claims that had been filed on Forest Service land, and then they set out to prepare the area and their ranger stations for transfer to the National Park administrators. Toward the end of October, the weather turned miserable and they rode for home. Blackened snags, half buried in snow, with embers still glowing reminded them of the summer just past.

Aftermath of the 1910 fires. PHOTOGRAPH BY R. H. MCKAY. USDA FOREST SERVICE REGION 1 ARCHIVES.

A Silent Farewell

On November first, Frank went to Kalispell to check in with Supervisor Haines at Forest Service Headquarters. *Haines advised me to move to Kalispell, as I had to leave the old ranger station, on account of the Park.* Frank had known that his ranger district was one of the most awesomely beautiful creations of nature. He had wanted it removed from the tampering of men's politics and ambitions so that it would be preserved in its natural state. National park status would do that, but leaving it and turning its protection over to someone else didn't set well just the same. This was the country he left his family in Germany to find and explore. He loved the mountains, valleys, and glaciers, the rivers and streams. He felt a part of it.

As a ranger, he had protected it with unwavering dedication. He had built the ranger station. It was Frank and Lulu's first home, and two of his children spent their first days of life there.

Frank had expected this time to come and inwardly tried to prepare himself, but coming face-to-face with the reality knotted his gut. He took a silent moment to collect and resign himself to what had to be. Then, without complaint, he acknowledged what Haines had said.

In the next two weeks, Frank and Lulu packed all their belongings, loaded them on Frank Kelly's gasoline launch, and shipped them down to Apgar. Then they loaded everything onto wagons to transport themselves and Jean and Frannie from Apgar to Belton where they took the Great Northern train to Kalispell.

When Frank arrived in Kalispell, he discovered that Supervisor Haines had been replaced by J. F. Preston. *Preston said that I wouldn't have no work all winter.* Thus, Frank's employment with the Forest Service was temporarily terminated.

Return to Service

Frank sat out the winter months in Kalispell, then early in 1911, he took the Bureau of Entomology's written exam and was assigned as a field agent under Chief Entomologist Joseph Brunner. Brunner had been a ranger, knew Frank, and was pleased to hire him. The job paid $90 a month and subsistence.

Frank worked that year near Lake McDonald studying and marking timber that had to be cut and the bark peeled in order to destroy the larva of the White Pine Beetle that had infested the pines in that area. At that time, fire and insects were the great killers of the forest. Later that year, he worked at Swan Lake helping to destroy insects that had infested timber there.

In 1912, Frank was reappointed to the Forest Service as a forest guard. He was stationed on Tally Lake in the Blackfeet National Forest, looking after trails and fires. In the fall, he surveyed and marked insect-infested timber, and that winter he was assigned to the Trego Ranger Station at Trego, Montana, to mark timber for railroad ties and supervise the cutting. He worked there until 1916, then transferred to the Pend Orielle Forest.

A Flathead National Forest ranger meeting, 1928. Standing, left to right: Mendenhall, Neitzling, Wiles, Ready, Thompson, Austin, Hornby, Diehl, R. Hutchinson, Hash. Squatting, left to right: Marsh, Sloan, Henry Thol, Frank Liebig, Hutchinson, Adams. U.S. FOREST SERVICE PHOTOGRAPH. LIEBIG COLLECTION.

Frank Liebig surveying damage after a forest fire. LIEBIG COLLECTION.

In 1917, he returned to the Flathead National Forest as a scaler. When he was not working as a scaler, he spent his time making maps and gathering the wild plants of the region for studies of their value as forage for game and stock.

By 1919, he had worked his way back up the Forest Service ladder and was assigned as district ranger at Coram, which included the old Belton Ranger District Headquarters that had been changed in 1909. In 1920 and until 1935, when Frank retired, he worked out of the headquarters at Kalispell serving as ranger-at-large in the Kootenai and Flathead Forests.

EIGHT

IN THE END, SHE MARKED HIM PAID

Frank had made himself at home in one of nature's empires. He suffered her fury and suppered on her bounty and lived quite a full life in her midst. But nature knows her worth and Frank had a debt to pay. He harnessed himself to the life of a forest ranger to hold back those who would waste her riches. He gathered specimens of her plants and grasses and flowers so that science might know her fragility, and for the sake of her history he mounted specimens of the birds and mammals of the region. He had taken something from her. He liked to think that he gave something in return and, in the end, she would mark him *paid*.

The rogue scientist gene in the Liebig woodsmen that had flourished in Frank's distant cousin Justus Liebig also rattled around in Frank, but not to the same effect. Justus gave himself to chemistry and the laboratory, discovered chloral, and revealed the importance of nitrogen, carbon, dioxide, and minerals to plant growth. Frank stuck to the woods and made his contribution to the study of plants from the hilltops. It was the job of the ranger to collect grasses and shrubs to assist the Department of Agriculture in determining the usefulness of certain species for livestock and wildlife. Frank went further. The collections were not just a part of his job. They were samples of his relationship with the wilderness. He knew the plants, flowers, and grasses well, and he helped others to get acquainted. He took courses in botany and collected, studied, and classified the plants and grasses of Glacier and the Flathead and Kootenai Forests, providing previously unidentified specimens to the Department of Agriculture. His collections were given to the University of Montana. They are particularly valued because of the growing interest in the biodiversity of Montana. His collections are of plant life prior to 1920 and include some rare and endangered species.

Since Frank had struck up a long-lasting friendship with the wild lands, his studies of nature were on a rather personal basis. Just how much so is revealed in this story by Don Bunger. Don met Frank Liebig in 1930 while he was working that summer for the Forest Service. Frank was fifty-eight years old. He had been a man of the wilderness for thirty-five years, six years on his own, eight years as a forest reserve ranger in Glacier, one year as a field agent with the Bureau of Entomology, and twenty years as a ranger in the Kootenai and Flathead Forests. He was as wiry and rugged as he was in his youth; few could keep up with him on the trail, few tried. Don remembers their meeting.

> *I worked the summer of 1930 building trails for the Forest Service. Our camp was situated south of Nyack and south of the highway on the Middle Fork of the Flathead River. One evening as we approached our campsite, after a long, hard day in the forests, we noticed a new white tent pitched near ours. Someone made the statement that we had company. A small man with a heavy mustache was busying himself about the tent. He introduced himself as Frank Liebig. Nothing of importance stood out about the man, but as we were helping carry in his duffel, we noticed that he had a bed with springs, which meant that he was a big shot of the forest. No one in our camp had been lucky enough to have a bed to sleep in. We made ours on the ground with fir boughs. When the cook yelled for supper the new man came in and had his meal with us. He answered all questions asked him, but nothing significant came out during the meal. After we ate, he went into his tent and brought out a big watermelon. That was the one and only melon we had all summer and it was thoroughly enjoyed by everyone. The melon increased our estimation of the*

man but he seemed to want to be alone. He went to his tent and so we went to ours.

As early as we would get up and before we went to work, he would be seen going over the trails. He came in with his arms and hands filled with grasses, weeds and flowers of all kinds. When we asked him what these were for, he replied that he was making a study of all the forage of that region and determining the usefulness for feed for game as well as domestic stock.

A week or two went by and no one penetrated the shell that seemed to be about him. Late one night he came into our camp looking for matches. I happened to be reading a book called Immesee, *written in German, and having a very slow time of it. Liebig noticed that I was reading and asked what it was. When I told him the title he said that was his favorite book as a boy. He asked me into his tent saying he would help me read it and help me with my German. "You see," said he, "German is my native tongue, I was born there." The story in* Immesee *became ever so much more delightful as Liebig read it aloud.*

He was having a wonderful time and so was I. Through this book and our enjoyment of it, we became close friends.

I will never forget the days that followed as we traveled over the trails together and sat about his campfire each evening after the work for the day was done. I needed only to listen as he poured out his knowledge of nature and answered all the questions I could think to ask. His face beamed with enjoyment. He knew he had found an interested listener.

Frank spent his time about camp searching for different flowers and grasses, looking them up in his little book and placing them in between big sheets of blotting paper. He had hundreds of them that he had gathered at or around camp and had been doing this all his life. He had specimens of every kind of flower, grass and weed in the area. I did not know just how much to heart he took this classification until I went on a fishing trip with him one day. The flowers were blooming on all sides and I kept asking the names of this and that flower. Each time he gave me the common name along with the scientific or Latin name. He did this without any reference to the book that he carried. I finally asked about a flower that was a fleabane, and he began to explain the difference between the greater and the lesser fleabane. Now these belong to a composite family of which there is probably five thousand members. So I asked how could any one person remember all the names of the composite family both common and scientific, if one family had as many as five thousand members?

"That's easy," Frank said, "They are my friends. I have worked with them for years. They are just like the Jones and the Smiths you know, maybe a dozen different Smiths. They are all different and have different first names. There is not one exactly like the other. Do you get their names mixed up when you speak to them? If you did you would feel badly and they would not take you as their friend for long. So, I work with these flowers, they are my friends, and I would feel badly if I were to misname them. I want that they continue being my friends so I make careful study and am sure that I name them all correctly. As I go along the trails I love to speak to my friends, and I do so in their first names or their common name, then I add the scientific name and there are very few that are slighted unless it is some very rare specimen that I have not had the pleasure of meeting for some time. When I speak to these rare flowers that one so seldom sees I always say, howdy stranger, I would like to make your acquaintance. Are you new in this region, or have you lived here for some time and we have never met? My name is Frank Liebig and yours—? I wait for a spell, they sometimes will be remembered, but if I can't remember I always carry this little book and we soon get acquainted after I have looked up the name. If I can't find them in my book then I find what family they belong to and give them a name. Then I promise that I will be sure to know that flower the next time we meet. I never like to break my promises, so I remember."

There was never before or since a man that could say he had so many friends and name them all. I wonder if his spirit is dwelling there on the mountainside speaking to his friends with each soft breeze that passes by, and the flowers nod their heads to return his greeting.

Frank's contribution to scientific studies was not limited to plants and flowers. He appears to have been apprehensive about the march of time on the wilderness. He was compelled to have many of the mammals he had shot submitted for scientific study or mounted so their form and regal beauty would be preserved for the eyes of the generations that would follow.

Frank was a hunter of some renown. He was never wildly pleased about a kill nor was he ever ashamed. He considered himself a brother of the wilderness and hunted according to a strict personal code. He killed whatever threatened his camp and what he needed to eat. Bear meat was his main diet, and he had shot many of them during his early years in Glacier.

Frank provided many of the grizzly skulls to Dr. Merriam of the Smithsonian Institute for study of these great creatures. He also had a great respect for the grace, beauty, and society of birds. He generally enjoyed just watching them. He took pictures of the rare birds in the region and sent them to Dr. Merriam for identification and historical documentation. He also took it upon himself to methodically collect and mount specimens of many of the birds of the region. He learned the craft of taxidermy and mounted the birds himself. He hired a Mr. Stanford in Kalispell to mount the mammals. His obsession for preserving the specimens in the same intricate detail that nature had produced them made his collection exceptional for historical study and museum display. His collection of birds and mammals of the Glacier region was shipped to San Francisco in 1915 for display at the Panama-Pacific Exposition. The collection was awarded World Silver and Bronze medals. Lulu donated the collection to Glacier National Park in 1952.

Retired Ranger Liebig showing his bird specimens to a group of children. LIEBIG COLLECTION.

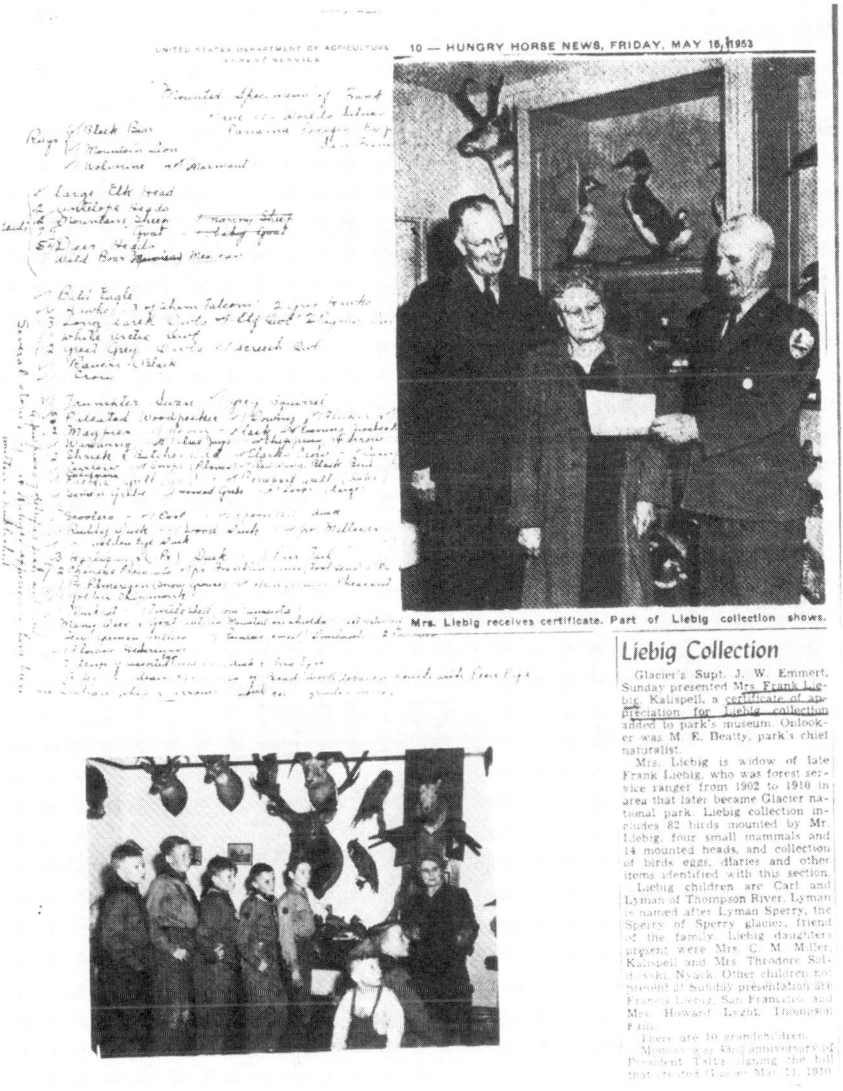

10 — HUNGRY HORSE NEWS, FRIDAY, MAY 15, 1953

Mrs. Liebig receives certificate. Part of Liebig collection shows.

Liebig Collection

Glacier's Supt. J. W. Emmert, Sunday presented Mrs. Frank Liebig, Kalispell, a certificate of appreciation for Liebig collection added to park's museum. Onlooker was M. E. Beatty, park's chief naturalist.

Mrs. Liebig is widow of late Frank Liebig, who was forest service ranger from 1902 to 1910 in area that later became Glacier national park. Liebig collection includes 82 birds mounted by Mr. Liebig, four small mammals and 14 mounted heads, and collection of birds eggs, diaries and other items identified with this section.

Liebig children are Carl and Lyman of Thompson River. Lyman is named after Lyman Sperry, the Sperry of Sperry glacier, friend of the family. Liebig daughters present were Mrs. C. M. Miller, Kalispell and Mrs. Throdore Soldowski, Nyack. Other children not present at Sunday presentation are Francis Liebig, San Francisco and Mrs. Howard Lyght, Thompson Falls.

There are 10 grandchildren.

Monday was 43rd anniversary of President Taft's signing the bill that created Glacier May 11, 1910.

Hungry Horse News article featuing Glacier National Park Superintendent J. S. W. Emmert presenting a certificate of appreciation to Lulu Liebig for the family's donation of Frank's animal and bird specimens.

HUNGRY HORSE NEWS. LIEBIG COLLECTION.

ATTRACTIVE WALK-IN DIORAMA is feature at Apgar Visitor Center in Glacier National Park. Artist is Helen Huck Voelker Ramon of the North Fork and Kalispell. Birds are from the Liebig collection donated to the park in the 1950s by Mrs. Frank Liebig. Her husband, early day forester, in what is now Glacier Park, mounted the birds.

Apgar Center Features Displays

ATTRACTIVE WALK-IN DIORAMA Glacier Park. Artist of production completed in 1975 was Helen Huck Voelker Ramon. Birds are from Liebig collection mounted by late Frank Liebig, early day forester in what is now Glacier Park

The *Hungry Horse News* reported on Frank's animal and plant specimens on display at the Apgar Center. HUNGRY HORSE NEWS. LIEBIG COLLECTION.

NINE

RANGER AGAIN FOR A DAY

Frank Liebig and Fred Herrig shared the bond of similar life experiences, from their childhoods in the German Empire to their cowboy days in the badlands and through the years as rangers in the American northwest. They respected each other's grit, and they were good friends.

Fred Herrig retired from the Forest Service in 1927 when he was sixty-seven years old. He had twenty-seven years of service as a ranger. He stayed in Fortine, used his pension money to help out his son and stepsons and their families during the Depression years, played checkers, told Spanish-American War stories at the local cafe, and gave advice to new rangers.

Frank Liebig retired in 1935 with thirty-three years of service. He was sixty-three. He stayed in Kalispell and took odd jobs landscaping and was often a volunteer scout leader, taking children on study trips into the wilderness.

In 1939, Frank went to Fortine to visit his old friend. Fred was seventy-nine then and having a hard time of it. He was crippled from long years in the saddle, arthritis, and a fall. He was in a wheelchair and the confinement plagued him. They spent the afternoon swapping stories about their lives and times. They were old men and each yearned to roll back time and be a ranger again, if only for a day; to once again wear a ranger's badge and hat, carry a rifle, a double-bitted axe, and a crosscut saw. To have a rolled blanket and slicker tied to the back of the saddle on a surefooted horse and a string of mules packed up heavy or light strung along behind. To once more enjoy the tangle of new trails ahead, the peaceful days, the lonesome nights, the blizzards and fires and tourists in trouble. Those were the days! They were grand, and for these two aging rangers they were gone. Gone, except in fond memory and in stories retold.

Fred died that year on May 17. The Spanish-American War Veterans of Kalispell paid tribute with a military burial service. A 7,250-foot-high mountain in the Stillwater State Forest in the Whitefish Mountain Range was named Herrig Mountain to honor him, and Herrig Creek runs through Pleasant Valley, near Marion, Montana.

Fred Herrig at home.
GREAT FALLS TRIBUNE.

Frank Liebig.
LIEBIG COLLECTION.

In his youth, Frank had been a rugged man who enjoyed the hearty challenge of the wilderness and the fragile splendor of the flowers of the mountains and fields. In old age, he was still wiry and forceful, but he was no longer as strong. He made fewer and fewer trips into the wild lands. Instead, he created some of the beauty of the mountains in his garden at home. One day in 1950, he was digging in the garden. Lulu watched from the kitchen window. The sky above was soft blue, cotton clouds drifted by, and a red-tailed hawk floated on the wind. Frank raised himself from the digging to watch the bird in flight. He fell and struck his head on the cement walk. He was seventy-eight and gone on to a new wilderness. Lulu joined him in 1966.

An 8,057-foot mountain east of Hungry Horse Reservoir in Montana's Great Bear Wilderness is named Mount Liebig in honor of this first ranger.

GLOSSARY AND PLACE NAMES

Altyn: Named for Dave Greenwood Altyn, financial backer of the Cracker Lake Mine.

Apgar: Named for Milo B. Apgar, among the first to arrive in the Lake McDonald region. He settled at the foot of the lake in the area that today bears his name.

Belton: Originally a temporary stop for the Great Northern Railway. The town had its beginnings as a box car. There are at least three accounts of who the town was named for. One declares the town was named for an early trapper, James Belton. The other accounts both claim that the town was named for the railroad's camp cook, who was either Andrew Belton or Daniel Bell, giving it the name Bell's Town or Bel'ton. Later renamed and is now West Glacier.

Belly River: The Blackfeet name for this area is Mokowanis, which translates as Big Belly and, according to Jack Holterman in *Place Names of Glacier/Waterton National Parks*, refers to the digestive tract of bison.

Camas Lakes: Named for the camas plant surrounding the lakes.

Chaney Glacier: Named by Dr. Lyman B. Sperry after Professor L. W. Chaney, a geologist from Carleton College in Northfield, Minnesota, who accompanied Sperry on a trip in 1895 and actually went out on the glacier.

Crosscut saw: A hand-operated saw with teeth specially designed and honed for cutting across the grain of wood.

Cruising timber: A survey to estimate the quantity and quality of timber in an area, according to tree species.

Double-bit axe: An axe with a cutting edge on both sides of the head.

Fire boss: The person responsible for all the activities to suppress a fire, and the support services at the fire.

Firebreak: A barrier to control the spread of fire. In Frank's time, it was generally a cleared strip or ditch dug with hand tools. Today, firebreaks are often created with small bulldozers.

Footage: The amount of lumber expressed in board feet. A board foot is a piece of lumber one foot square and one inch thick or its equivalent volume in other sizes.

Forester: Anyone engaged in the profession of forestry. At the turn of the century it was applied only to forest officials. Today, the term usually refers to college-trained professionals.

Forest guard: Typically a local resident who assisted the ranger in locating and putting out fires. Often laid off in winter when fire danger was low.

Forest ranger: A U.S. Civil Service officer appointed to be in charge of a unit of forest land. Responsible for enforcing the programs and policies of the U.S. Forest Service in his or her district.

Forestry: The science, art, and practice of managing and using the natural resources that occur on, in, and with forest lands.

Forest squatter: A person living in a forest without official right or permission.

Gunsight Pass: Named by George Bird Grinnell for its resemblance to the rear sight of a rifle. Gunsight Mountain, just northwest of the pass, was originally named Mount Comeau after Denny Comeau, a settler at Lake McDonald and favorite guide of Dr. Sperry. Comeau Pass lies just west of Gunsight Mountain.

Kintla Lakes: *Kintla* is the Kootenai word for "sack." Once you got in, you could not get out. The name resulted from a tribal story about an Indian who fell into the lake and disappeared.

Lake McDonald: There are at least two likely versions of how the lake was named. One is that Duncan McDonald, son of Hudson Bay Company's factor Angus McDonald, camped near the lake while on a trip to Canada and carved his name in the bark of a tree. Early settlers saw the etched name on the tree and began calling the lake "McDonald's." Another version included in the papers of historian L. O. Vaught claims the lake was named after trapper John McDonald who, in the 1880s, had built a cabin nearby where he ran his trap lines. He was well known in the Flathead Valley and the lake became known as McDonald's Lake.

Lookout: A person employed to watch for and report wildland fires from a vantage point. Also, the tower located at the vantage point.

Lumber tally: A record of lumber volume, by boards or pieces, by size, grade, and species.

Mattock: A digging tool with two blades set at right angles to the handle. One blade is usually a hoe-like adze, and the other blade is either a pointed pick or a small axe.

National forest: A federal reservation administered, protected and managed by the U.S. Department of Agriculture Forest Service, under a program of multiple use, sustained yield for timber, range, wildlife, water, and outdoor recreational purposes.

National park: A federal reservation administered by the U.S. Department of the Interior National Park Service to conserve the scenery, the flora and fauna, and any natural and historic objects within the boundaries for public enjoyment in perpetuity.

Palouser: A lantern made with a large tin can (lard/tomato or two-pound coffee can) with a candle set in it. The candle flame reflects brightly off the tin, casts a good light, and will continue to burn even in a high wind. The name comes from the Palouse country in Washington state where a harvest hand who had to work steady through the night was said to have swapped his bed, which he never had time to use, for a lantern.

Pulaski: Firefighter's tool combining an axe on one side of the metal head and grub hoe on the other. Ranger Edward Crockett Pulaski, a hero of the 1910 fires in northern Idaho and western Montana, is credited with developing the tool.

Ranger-at-large: A ranger assigned to the headquarters of a national forest. Sent throughout a region to troubleshoot or perform a specific task.

Ranger district: An administrative subdivision of a national forest. In the early years, a district could include anywhere from a few hundred to a million acres.

Scaler: A timber worker who measures and reports the volume of logs and fuel wood.

Soogan: A logger's term for a blanket, often made from patches of pants or coats and used as a bedroll.

Sperry Glacier: Named for Professor Lyman B. Sperry from the University of Minnesota. He organized a party to explore the glacier in 1895.

Spot fire: A small fire distant from the main forest fire.

Stanton Mountain: Named for Mrs. Lottie Stanton, who in 1891 outclimbed some guests of guide Frank Geduhn, reaching the top of the peak that now bears her name before the rest of them.

Sherburne Lake: Named for Joe Sherburne, a well-known merchant in Browning, Montana. The Sherburnes owned oil and mining claims in the Swiftcurrent drainage.

Swiftcurrent Pass: Named by George Bird Grinnell in 1885. The name was originally applied to the stream and derived from the Cree term for "swift flowing river." After horse-stealing raids to the west, the Blackfeet would drive their plunder through the notch, earning it the early name Horse Thief Pass.

Waterton Lakes: Named for the English naturalist and explorer Charles Waterton by Captain T. W. Blakiston, who was a naturalist with the British Palliser Expedition from 1857 to 1859.

Windfall: A tree or trees or their branches broken and blown down by strong winds. Sometimes called blowdown or windthrow.

BIBLIOGRAPHY

Bowers, Maynard C. *Through The Years In Glacier National Park: An Administrative History*. Glacier Natural History Association. 1960.

Buchholtz, Curtis W. *Man In Glacier*. Glacier Natural History Association. 1976. "The Last Summer at Lake McDonald." *Montana, The Magazine of Western History*. Autumn, 1976.

Bunger, Donald. *The Liebig Story*. Unpublished manuscript.

Cannon, Carol. "Whatever Became of Old Ant Flat?" *Montana, Magazine of the Northern Rockies*. Winter, 1973.

Dusenberry, Verne. *The Montana Cree, A Study in Religious Persistence*. First edition, Aimquist and Wiksell, 1962. Second edition, University of Oklahoma Press. 1998.

Ford-Robertson, F. C., editor. *Terminology of Forest Science, Technology, Practice and Products*. Society of American Foresters. 1971.

Frome, Michael. *The Forest Service*. Praeger Publishing Inc. 1971.

Garraty, John A. and Peter Gay. *The Columbia History of the World*. Harper & Row. 1972.

Gildart, Robert C. (Bert). "Montana's Early-Day Rangers." *Montana Magazine*. 1985.

Herrig, Frederick. Letters and memorabilia.

Herrig, Frederick. Interview titled; "President Roosevelt calls an Old Acquaintance of the Plains out of the Crowd." *The Anaconda Standard*. May 31, 1903.

Herrig, Frederick, "Roosevelt as a Ranchman." McClure Syndicate. October 23, 1898.

Holloway, Garrett B. "Golden Anniversary of Fiery Horror Occasions Thoughtful Reappraisal." *Montana, The Magazine of Western History*. Autumn, 1960. Pp. 49–54.

Johnson, Olga W. "Montana's First Forest Rangers Experienced One Hectic Thing After Another In Woods." *Great Falls Tribune*. August 8, 1954.

Liebig, Frank F. "1944 letter." *Early Days In The Forest Service*, Vol I. U.S. Forest Service. 1944. Various documents and personal papers.

Miss, Christian J., editor. Northwest Archaeological Associates, Inc. *Historic Overview of the Kootenai National Forest*. U.S. Forest Service. May 25, 1994.

Morris, Edmund. *The Rise of Theodore Roosevelt*. Ballantine Books. April, 1980.

Presidential proclamations. *Flathead and Lewis and Clark Reserves*. Washington D.C. #29, #31, February 22, 1897; #3, June 9, 1903; and March 2, 1907.

Reynolds, George W., Information Specialist, U.S. Forest Service, Northern Region. "Nature Sets the Stage as Defeated Men Pray for Quenching Rains." *Montana, The Magazine of Western History*. Autumn, 1960.

Robinson, Donald H., Asst. Chief Park Naturalist at Glacier National Park. *Throughout the Years In Glacier National Park*. Glacier Natural History Association. May, 1960.

Roosevelt, Theodore. *Rough Riders*. Corner House Publishers. 1979. Original copyright: Chas. Scribner's Sons. 1899.

Roosevelt, Theodore. "Western Spirit as Roosevelt Learned it from Men he Worked with on the Range." Outlook Company, reprinted in *Spokesman-Review*. July 6, 1913.

Shaw, Charlie. *The Flathead Story*. U.S. Forest Service. 1967.

Soldowski, Jean Liebig. Notes and interviews.

Trinka, Zdena. *Medora*. International Book Publishers. 1940.

ABOUT THE AUTHOR

C. W. (Carol) Guthrie's love affair with the Glacier area began when she and her dad drove the Going-to-the-Sun Road when she was nine years old. For the past twenty-five years, following a career working for the U.S. Air Force, she has explored the park and its history and authored or co-authored five books about the park, including *All Aboard! for Glacier: The Great Northern Railway and Glacier National Park; Death & Survival in Glacier National Park: True Tales of Tragedy, Courage, & Misadventure; Glacier National Park: The First 100 Years; Glacier National Park Legends and Lore: Along Going-to-the-Sun Road;* and *Going-to-the-Sun Road: Glacier National Park's Highway to the Sky.*

More Glacier National Park History with Author

C. W. Guthrie

Death & Survival
in Glacier National Park

Written by career experts on Glacier Park and featuring accurate and in-depth accounts of vacations cut short by harrowing tragedy, near-death survival, and hair-raising rescues. Includes historical photographs and the most complete chronology of all 296 deaths in the park to date.

978-1-56037-658-3 $18.95

All Aboard! for Glacier:
The Great Northern Railway and Glacier National Park

Original photographs, posters, menus, and postcards complement this lively history of the creation and promotion of Glacier National Park by the "Empire Builder" Great Northern Railway.

978-1-56037-276-9 $15.95

Glacier National Park: The First 100 Years

Guthrie details the remarkable geologic and human history of this unmatched and storied land, then profiles Glacier National Park decade by decade.

978-1-56037-336-0 $39.95

Going-to-the-Sun Road:
Glacier National Park's Highway to the Sky

Excellent historical and contemporary photographs complement this history of the construction of Glacier National Park's remarkable Going-to-the-Sun Road.

978-1-56037-335-3 $12.95